W9-DBM-368

Editor
Dona Herweck Rice

Editorial Project Manager
Dona Herweck Rice

Editor-in-Chief
Sharon Coan, M.S. Ed.

Illustrator
Kevin Barnes

Cover Artist
Barb Lorseyedi

Art Coordinator
Kevin Barnes

Imaging
Alfred Lau
James Edward Grace
Rosa C. See

Product Manager
Phil Garcia

Publishers
Rachelle Cracchiolo, M.S. Ed.
Mary Dupuy Smith, M.S. Ed.

Comprehension & Critical Thinking
LEVEL 4

Includes Document-Based Questions

Author

Jennifer Overend Prior

Reading passages provided by *TIME For Kids* magazine.

Teacher Created Materials, Inc.
6421 Industry Way
Westminster, CA 92683
www.teachercreated.com

ISBN-0-7439-3374-5

©2002 Teacher Created Materials, Inc.
Reprinted, 2003
Made in U.S.A.

Table of Contents

Introduction

Comprehension is the primary goal of any reading task. Students who comprehend what they read have more opportunities in life as well as better test performance. Through the use of interesting grade-level nonfiction passages followed by exercises that require vital reading and thinking skills, *Comprehension and Critical Thinking* will help you to develop confident readers who can demonstrate their knowledge on standardized tests. In addition you will promote the comprehension necessary to form the basis for a lifetime of learning.

The articles in *Comprehension and Critical Thinking* present facts about the contemporary world as well as the past. A document-based question for each passage gives your students practice in the newest trend in standardized testing. The students respond to a critical-thinking question based on the information gleaned from a given document. This document is related to the passage it accompanies. Document-based questions show a student's ability to apply prior knowledge and his or her capacity to transfer knowledge to a new situation.

The activities are time-efficient, allowing students to practice these skills every week. To yield the best results, such practice must begin at the start of the school year.

Students will need to use test-taking skills and strategies throughout their lives. The exercises in *Comprehension and Critical Thinking* will guide your students to become better readers *and* test-takers. After practicing the exercises in this book, you will be pleased with your students' comprehension performance, not only on standardized tests, but with *any* expository text they encounter within the classroom and beyond its walls.

Readability

All of the passages have a 4.0–4.9 reading level based on the Flesch Kincaid Readability Formula. This formula determines the readability level by calculating the number of words, syllables, and sentences.

Preparing Students to Read Nonfiction Text

One of the best ways to prepare students to read expository text is to read a short selection aloud to them daily. Reading expository text aloud is critical to developing your students' ability to read it themselves. Since making predictions is another way to make students tap into their prior knowledge, read the beginning of a passage, then stop, and ask them to predict what might occur next. Do this at several points throughout your reading of the text. By doing this, over time you will find that your students' ability to make accurate predictions greatly increases.

Of course, talking about nonfiction concepts is also very important. Remember, however, that discussion can never replace reading aloud because people rarely speak using the vocabulary and complex sentence structures of written language.

Questions help students, especially struggling readers, to focus on what is important in a text. Also, remember the significance of wait time. Research has shown that the amount of time an educator waits for a student to answer after posing a question has a critical effect on learning. So, after you ask a student a question, silently count to five (or ten if you have a student who struggles to get his or her thoughts into words) before giving any additional prompts or redirecting the question to another student.

Introduction *(cont.)*

Bloom's Taxonomy

The questions that follow each passage in *Comprehension and Critical Thinking* assess all levels of learning by following Bloom's Taxonomy, a six-level classification system for comprehension questions devised by Benjamin Bloom in 1956. The questions that follow each passage are always presented in order, progressing from knowledge to evaluation.

The skills listed for each level are essential to keep in mind when teaching comprehension to ensure that your students reach the higher levels of thinking. Use this classification to form your own questions whenever your students listen to or read material.

Level 1: Knowledge—Students recall information or find requested information in an article. They show memory of dates, events, places, people, and main ideas.

Level 2: Comprehension—Students understand information. This means that they can find information that is stated in a different way than the question. It also means students can rephrase or restate information in their own words.

Level 3: Application—Students apply their knowledge to a specific situation. They may be asked to do something new with the knowledge.

Level 4: Analysis—Students break things into their component parts and examine those parts. They notice patterns in information.

Level 5: Synthesis—Students do something new with the information. They pull knowledge together to create new ideas. They generalize, predict, plan, and draw conclusions.

Level 6: Evaluation—Students make judgments and assess value. They form an opinion and defend it. They can also understand another person's viewpoint.

Practice Suggestions

Do the first few passages and related questions with the whole class. Demonstrate your own metacognitive processes by thinking aloud about how to figure out an answer. This means that you essentially tell your students your thoughts as they come to you. For example, suppose the question is the following: "What would have happened to the baby dinosaurs if mud had not preserved them?" Tell the students all your thoughts as they occur to you, for example: "What happens to most animals' bodies when they die? Not every animal's body becomes a fossil. The mud is what preserved the dinosaurs' bodies. So, if the mud hadn't covered them, the bodies would probably have deteriorated or rotted away."

Short-answer Questions

Many of the questions require short answers. The students are asked to use information from the article to summarize, draw conclusions, identify hidden meanings, etc. The student should support his or her ideas and opinions when necessary.

Introduction *(cont.)*

Document-based Questions

It is especially important to guide your students in how to understand, interpret, and respond to the document-based questions. For these questions, in order to formulate a response the students will have to rely on their prior knowledge and common sense in addition to the information provided in the document. Again, the best way to teach this is to demonstrate through thinking aloud how to figure out an answer. Since these questions are usually interpretive, you can allow for some variation in student responses.

The more your students practice, the more competent and confident they will become. Plan to have the class do every exercise in *Comprehension and Critical Thinking*. If you have some students who cannot read the articles independently, allow them to read with a partner, then work through the comprehension questions alone. Eventually all students must practice reading and answering the questions independently. Move to this stage as soon as possible. For the most effective practice sessions, follow these steps:

1. Have the students read the text silently and answer the questions.

2. Have the students exchange papers to correct each other's multiple choice section.

3. Collect all the papers to score the short-answer question and the document-based question portion.

4. Return the papers to their owners and discuss how the students determined their answers.

5. Refer to the exact wording in the passage.

6. Point out how students had to use their background knowledge to answer certain questions.

7. Discuss how a child should explain his or her stance in each short-answer question.

8. Discuss the document-based question thoroughly.

Scoring the Practice Passages

With the students, use the "number correct" approach to scoring the practice passages, especially since this coincides with the student achievement graph on page 109. However, for your own records and to share with the parents, you may want to keep track of numeric scores for each student. If you choose to do this, do not write the numeric score on the paper.

Standardized Test Success

One of the key objectives of *Comprehension and Critical Thinking* is to prepare your students to get the best possible scores on the reading portion of standardized tests. A student's ability to do well on traditional standardized tests in comprehension requires these factors:

- a large vocabulary
- test-taking skills
- the ability to cope with stress effectively

Introduction *(cont.)*

Test-taking Skills

Every student in your class needs instruction in test-taking skills. Even fluent readers and logical thinkers will perform better on standardized tests if you provide instruction in the following areas.

Understanding the question: Teach students to break down the question to figure out what is really being asked of them. This book will prepare them for the kinds of questions they will encounter on standardized tests.

Concentrating just on what the text says: Show students how to restrict their response to just what is asked. When you go over the practice passages, ask your students to show where they found the correct response in the text.

Ruling out distracters in multiple-choice answers: Teach students to look for the key words in a question and look for those specific words to find the information in the text. They also need to know that they may have to look for synonyms for the key words.

Maintaining concentration: Use classroom time to practice this in advance. Reward students for maintaining concentration. Explain to them the purpose of this practice and the reason why concentration is so essential.

Practice environmental conditions throughout the year in order to acclimate your students to the testing environment. For example, if your students' desks are usually together, have students move them apart whenever you practice so it won't feel strange on the test day.

Some other ideas for "setting the stage" whenever you practice include the following:

- Put a "Testing–Do Not Disturb" sign on the door.
- Require no talking, active listening, and following directions during practice sessions.
- Provide a small strip of construction paper for each student to use as a marker.
- Give each student two sharpened pencils and have a back-up supply handy. Tell the students to raise a broken pencil, and you will immediately provide them with a new one.

Coping with Stress

Teach students to recognize their apprehension and other stressful feelings associated with testing. Give students some suggestions for handling stress, such as taking a deep breath and stretching.

At the beginning of the school year start talking about good habits like getting enough rest, having a good breakfast, and daily exercise. Enlist parental support by sending home a letter encouraging parents to start these good habits right away.

Remember to let students stretch and move around between tests. Provide a physical release by running in place or playing "Simon Says" as a stress-buster during practice sessions throughout the year as well as on the test day.

Introduction *(cont.)*

Build confidence throughout the school year by using the practice passages in this book. Do not include the passage scores in the students' class grades. Instead, encourage your students by having them complete the achievement line graph on page 109, showing how many questions they answered correctly for each practice passage. Seeing their scores improve or stay consistently high over time will provide encouragement and motivation.

On the test day, promote a relaxed, positive outlook. Tell your students to visualize doing really well. Remind them that since they have practiced so much, they are thoroughly prepared.

Teaching Nonfiction Comprehension Skills

Nonfiction comprehension encompasses many skills that develop with a lot of practice. The following information offers you a brief overview of how to teach the crucial skills of recognizing text structure, visualizing, summarizing, and learning new vocabulary. This information is designed for your use with other classroom materials, not the practice passages in *Comprehension and Critical Thinking*.

You will find many of these skills in scope-and-sequence charts and standards for reading comprehension:

- recognizes stated main idea
- identifies details
- determines sequence
- recalls details
- labels parts
- summarizes
- identifies time sequence
- describes character
- retells information in own words
- classifies, sorts into categories
- compares and contrasts
- makes generalizations
- draws conclusions
- recognizes text organization
- predicts outcome and consequences
- experiences an emotional reaction to a text
- recognizes facts
- applies information to a new situation

Introduction (cont.)

Typical Comprehension Questions

Teaching the typical kinds of standardized test questions gives students an anticipation framework and helps them learn how to comprehend what they read. It also boosts their test scores. The questions generally found on standardized reading comprehension tests are as follows:

Facts—questions based on exactly what the text states: who, what, when, where, why, and how many

Sequence—questions based on order: what happened first, last, and in between

Conditions—questions asking students to compare, contrast, and find the similarities and differences

Summarizing—questions that require students to restate, paraphrase choose main ideas, conclude, and select a title

Vocabulary—questions based on word meaning, synonyms and antonyms, proper nouns, words in context, technical words, geographical words, and unusual adjectives

Outcomes—questions that ask readers to draw upon their own experiences or prior knowledge, which means that students must understand cause and effect, consequences, and implications

Opinion—questions that ask the author's intent and require the use of inferencing skills

Document-based—questions that require students to analyze information from a source document to draw a conclusion or form an opinion

Introduction (cont.)

Teaching Text Structure

Students lacking in knowledge of text structure are at a distinct disadvantage; yet this skill is sometimes overlooked in instruction. When referring to a piece to locate information to answer a question, understanding structure allows students to locate quickly the right area in which to look. Students also need to understand text structure in order to make predictions and improve overall comprehension.

Some children have been so immersed in print that they have a natural understanding of structure. For instance, they realize that the first sentence of a paragraph often contains the main idea, followed by details about that idea. But many students need direct instruction in text structure. The first step in this process is making certain that students know the way that authors typically present ideas in writing. This knowledge is a major asset for students.

Transitional paragraphs join together two paragraphs to make the writing flow. Most transitional paragraphs do not have a main idea. In all other paragraph types, there is a main idea, even if it is not stated. In the following examples the main idea is italicized. In order of frequency, the four types of expository paragraph structures are as follows:

1. **The main idea is often the first sentence of a paragraph. The rest of the paragraph provides the supporting details.**

   Clara Barton, known as America's first nurse, was a brave and devoted humanitarian. While caring for others, she was shot at, got frostbitten fingers, and burned her hands. She had severe laryngitis twice and almost lost her eyesight. Yet she continued to care for the sick and injured until she died at the age of 91.

2. **The main idea may fall in the center of the paragraph, surrounded on both sides by details.**

   The coral have created a reef where more than 200 kinds of birds and about 1,500 types of fish live. *In fact, Australia's Great Barrier Reef provides a home for many interesting animals.* These include sea turtles, giant clams, crabs, and crown-of-thorns starfish.

3. **The main idea comes at the end of the paragraph as a summary of the details that came before.**

   Each year Antarctica spends six months in darkness, from mid March to mid September. The continent is covered year-round by ice, which causes sunlight to reflect off its surface. It never really warms up. In fact, the coldest temperature ever recorded was in Antarctica. *Antarctica has one of the harshest environments in the world.*

4. **The main idea is not stated in the paragraph and must be inferred from the details given. This paragraph structure is the most challenging for primary students.**

   The biggest sea horse ever found was over a foot long. Large sea horses live along the coasts of New Zealand, Australia, and California. Smaller sea horses live off the coast of Florida, in the Caribbean Sea, and in the Gulf of Mexico. The smallest adult sea horse ever found was only one half-inch long!

Introduction *(cont.)*

In this example, the implied main idea is that sea horses' sizes vary based on where they live. Some other activities that will help your students understand text structure include the following:

Color code: While reading text, have your students use different colored pencils or highlighters to color code important elements such as the main idea (red), supporting details (yellow), causes (green) and effects (purple), facts (blue) and opinions (orange). When they have finished, ask them to describe the paragraph's structure in their own words.

Search the text: Teach students to identify the key words in a question and look specifically for those words in the passage. Then, when you discuss a comprehension question with the students, ask them, "Which words will you look for in the text to find the answer? If you can't find the words, can you find synonyms? Where will you look for the words?"

Signal words: There are specific words used in text that indicate, or signal, that the text has a cause and effect, sequence, or comparison structure. Teaching your students these words will greatly improve their ability to detect text structure and increase their comprehension.

These Signal Words	Indicate
since, because, caused by, as a result, before and after, so, this led to, if/then, reasons, brought about, so that, when/then, that's why	cause and effect The answer to "Why did it happen?" is a *cause*. The answer to "What happened?" is an *effect*.
first, second, third, next, then, after, before, last, later, since then, now, while, meanwhile, at the same time, finally, when, at last, in the end, since that time, following, on (date), at (time)	sequence
but, even if, even though, although, however, instead, not only, unless, yet, on the other hand, either/or, as well as, "–er" and "–st" words (such as better, best, shorter, tallest, bigger, smallest, most, worst)	compare/contrast

Introduction *(cont.)*

Teaching Visualization Skills

Visualization—seeing the words of a text as mental images in the mind—is a significant factor setting apart proficient readers from low-achieving ones. Studies have shown that the ability to generate vivid images while reading strongly correlates with a person's comprehension of text. However, research has also revealed that *20 percent of all children do not visualize or experience sensory images when reading*. These children are automatically handicapped in their ability to comprehend text, and they are usually the students who avoid and dislike reading because they never connect to text in a personal, meaningful way.

Active visualization can completely engross a reader in text. You have experienced this when you just could not put a book down, and you stayed up all night just to finish it. Skillful readers automatically weave their own memories into text as they read to make personalized, lifelike images. In fact, every person develops a unique interpretation of any text. This personalized reading experience explains why most people prefer a book to its movie.

Visualization is not static; unlike photographs, these are "movies in the mind." Mental images must constantly be modified to incorporate new information as it is disclosed by the text. Therefore, your students must learn how to revise their images if they encounter information that requires them to do so.

Sensory imaging—employing any of the other senses besides sight—is closely related to visual imaging. It too has been shown to be crucial to the construction of meaning during reading. This is because the more senses that are employed in a task, the more neural pathways are built, resulting in more avenues to access information. You have experienced sensory imaging when you could almost smell the smoke of the forest fire, taste the sizzling bacon, or laughed along with a character as you read. Sensory imaging connects the reader personally and intimately to the text and breathes life into words.

Since visualization is a challenging skill for one out of every five students to develop, begin with simple *fictional* passages to scaffold their attempts and promote success. After your students have experienced success with visualization and sensory imaging in literature, they are ready to employ these techniques in nonfiction text.

Visualization has a special significance in nonfiction text. The technical presentation of ideas in nonfiction text coupled with new terms and concepts often overwhelm and discourage students.

Using visualization can help them to move beyond these barriers. As an added benefit, people who create mental images display better long-term retention of factual material.

Clearly there are important reasons to teach visualization and sensory imaging skills to your students. But perhaps the most compelling reason is this: Visualizing demands active involvement, turning passive students into active constructors of meaning.

Doing Think-alouds

It is essential for you to introduce visualization by doing think-alouds to describe your own visualization of text. To do this, read aloud the first one or two lines of a passage and describe what images come to your mind. Be sure to include *details that were not stated in the text,* such as the house has two stories and green shutters. Then read the next two lines and explain how you add to or otherwise modify your image based on the new information provided by the text.

Introduction *(cont.)*

When you are doing a think-aloud for your class, be sure to do the following:

- Explain how your images help you to better understand the passage.

- Describe details, being sure to include some from your own schema.

- Mention the use of your senses—the more the better.

- Describe your revision of the images as you read further and encounter new information.

Teaching Summarizing and Paraphrasing

Summarizing informational text is a crucial skill for students to master. It is also one of the most challenging. Summarizing means pulling out *only* the essential elements of a passage—just the main idea and supporting details. Research has shown that having students put information into their own words causes it to be processed more thoroughly. Thus, paraphrasing increases both understanding and long-term retention of material. Information can be summarized through such diverse activities as speaking, writing, drawing, or creating a project.

The basic steps of summarizing are as follows:

- Look for the paragraph's main idea sentence; if there is none, create one.

- Find the supporting details, being certain to group all related terms or ideas.

- Record information that is repeated or restated only once.

- Put the summary together into an organized format.

Scaffolding is of critical importance. Your students will need a lot of modeling, guided practice, and small group or partner practice before attempting to summarize independently. All strategies should be done as a whole group and then with a partner several times before letting the students do it on their own. Encourage the greatest transfer of knowledge by modeling each strategy's use in multiple content areas.

Teaching Vocabulary

In the early years, students may start seeing words in print that they may have never met before in either print or oral language. As a result, these students need direct instruction in vocabulary to make real progress toward becoming readers who can independently access expository text. Teaching the vocabulary that occurs in a text significantly improves comprehension. Since students encounter vocabulary terms in science, social studies, math, and language arts, strategies for decoding and understanding new words must be taught throughout the day.

Students' vocabularies develop following this progression: listening, speaking, reading, and writing. This means that a child understands a word when it is spoken to him long before he uses it in his own speaking. The child will also understand the word when he reads it before he will attempt to use it in his own writing. Each time a child comes across the same word, his or her understanding of that word deepens. Research has shown that vocabulary instruction has the most positive effect on reading comprehension when students encounter the words multiple times. That is why the best vocabulary instruction requires students to use new words in writing and speaking as well as in reading.

Introduction *(cont.)*

Teaching vocabulary can be both effective and fun, especially if you engage the students' multiple modalities (listening, speaking, reading, and writing). In addition, instruction that uses all four modalities is most apt to reach every learner.

The more experience a child has with language, the stronger his or her vocabulary base. Therefore, the majority of vocabulary activities should be done as whole group or small group instruction. In this way children with a limited vocabulary can learn from their peers' knowledge base and will find vocabulary activities less frustrating. Remember, too, that a picture is worth a thousand words. Whenever possible provide a picture of a new vocabulary word.

Selecting Vocabulary Words to Study

Many teachers feel overwhelmed when teaching vocabulary because they realize that it is impossible to thoroughly cover all students' unknown words. Do not attempt to study every unknown word. Instead, choose the words from each selection wisely. Following these guidelines will result in an educationally sound vocabulary list:

1. First, choose words that are critical to the article's meaning.

2. Then, choose conceptually difficult words.

3. Finally, choose words with the greatest utility value—those that you anticipate the children will see more often (*e.g.,* choose *anxious* rather than *appalled*).

These suggestions are given for teaching nonfiction material in general. *Do not select and preteach vocabulary from these practice passages.* You want to simulate real test conditions in which the children would have no prior knowledge of any of the material in any of the passages.

Elements of Effective Vocabulary Instruction

Vocabulary instruction is only effective if children permanently add the concepts to their knowledge base. Research has shown that the most effective vocabulary program includes contextual, structural, and classification strategies. You can do this by making certain that your vocabulary instruction includes the following elements:

- using context clues
- knowing the meaning of affixes (prefixes, suffixes) and roots
- introducing new words as synonyms and antonyms of known words

Introduction *(cont.)*

Using Context Clues

Learning vocabulary in context is important for two reasons. First, it makes children become active in determining word meanings, and second, it transfers into their lives by offering them a way to figure out unknown words in their independent reading. If you teach your students how to use context clues, you may eventually be able to omit preteaching any vocabulary that is defined in context (so long as the text is written at your students' independent level). There are five basic kinds of context clues.

1. **Definition:** The easiest case is when the definition is given elsewhere in the sentence or paragraph.

   example: The ragged, *tattered* dress hung from her shoulders.

2. **Synonym:** Another simple case is when a synonym or synonymous phrase is immediately used.

   example: Although she was fat, her *obesity* never bothered her until she went to middle school.

3. **Contrast:** The meaning may be implied through contrast to a known word or concept. Be alert to these words that signal contrast: although, but, however, even though.

   example: Although Adesha had always been *prompt*, today he was 20 minutes late.

4. **Summary:** Another form is summary, which sums up a list of attributes.

   example: Tundra, desert, grassland, and rain forest are four of the Earth's *biomes*.

5. **Mood:** Sometimes the meaning can be grasped from the mood of the larger context in which it appears. The most difficult situation is when the meaning must be inferred with few other clues.

   example: Her *shrill* voice was actually making my ears hurt.

Your general approach to building vocabulary should include the following:

Brainstorming: Students brainstorm a list of words associated with a familiar word, sharing everyone's knowledge and discussing unfamiliar words thoroughly.

Semantic mapping: Students sort the brainstormed words into categories, often creating a visual organization tool—such as a graphic organizer or word web—to depict the relationships.

Feature analysis: You provide key features and a list of terms in a chart, such as a semantic matrix or Venn diagram. Have students identify the similarities and differences between the items.

Synonyms and antonyms: Introducing both synonyms and antonyms for the terms you study provides a structure for meaning and substantially increases your students' vocabulary rapidly.

Analogies: Analogies are similar to synonyms but require higher-level thinking. The goal is to help students identify the relationship between words. Analogies appear on standardized tests in the upper elementary grades.

   example: Bark is to tree as skin is to <u>human</u>.

Word affixes: Studying common prefixes and suffixes will help students deduce new words, especially in context. Teach students to ask, "Does this look like any other word I know? Can I find any word parts I know? Can I figure out the meaning based on its context?"

Introduction *(cont.)*

Important Affixes for Primary Grades

Prefix	Meaning	Example	Suffix	Meaning	Example
un	not	unusual	**-s or -es**	more than one	cars; tomatoes
re	again	remake	**-ed**	did an action	raked
in, im	not	immature	**-ing**	doing an action	swimming
dis	opposite	displease	**-ly**	like, very	greatly
non	not	nonsense	**-er**	a person who	farmer
over	too much	overwhelm	**-ful**	full of	graceful
mis	bad	misuse	**-or**	a person who	creator
pre	before	predate	**-less**	without	careless
de	opposite	decompose	**-er**	more	taller
under	less	underachieve	**-est**	most	tallest

What a Winter!

The Ewen family awoke to a scary sight. A nearby creek was spilling over its banks. Soon the waters surrounded their home. The Ewens escaped by wading through deep water.

"I didn't expect it to come up that fast," says Melissa Ewen. The last time she saw their home, it was nearly covered with water. "Everything we own was in there—photos that can't be replaced."

During the winter of 1997–1998, strong winter storms slammed much of the U.S. Bad weather often hits at this time of year. This time there was a change in climate patterns. It was called El Niño and it made the storms even more dangerous than usual.

El Niño caused strange weather worldwide. "This is the weather event of the century," said James Baker.

Heavy rain began to pound California on February 1. The rain caused flash floods and mudslides. Huge waves crashed over beaches. Winds knocked out power to thousands of families.

At the same time, thunderstorms and tornadoes roared across Florida. They tossed around trees, roofs, and even small planes. Winds gusted to 100 miles an hour.

Then the storms moved north. Snow, rain, and wind battered much of the East Coast.

Scientists had been studying El Niño. The knew the wild weather would come. El Niño happens every few years. It is caused by winds and ocean currents traveling across the Pacific Ocean.

El Niño causes strange weather around the world. Places that usually receive a lot of rain may have droughts. Places that have little rain end up with heavy rains and flooding. This El Niño was the most powerful of the century.

El Niño affects more than weather. It warms up large bands of water in the Pacific Ocean. This confuses many living things. Fish and birds travel too far north. Sea lions in California starved because the fish they eat swam south.

El Niño was at its strongest in December. Much of the world felt its effects for months.

What a Winter! *(cont.)*

Directions: Answer these questions. You may look at the story.

1. What happened to the Ewen's home?

2. What is the name of the weather event?

3. What kinds of damage can storms cause?

4. Apply this experience to your own life. What would you do to protect yourself in a strong storm?

5. Why do you think scientists study El Niño?

6. How do you think Melissa felt during the flood? Why?

7. Make a list comparing the good and bad things El Niño brought to different areas of the world.

8. Summarize the information about El Niño.

What a Winter! *(cont.)*

Directions: Look at the diagrams. Answer the questions.

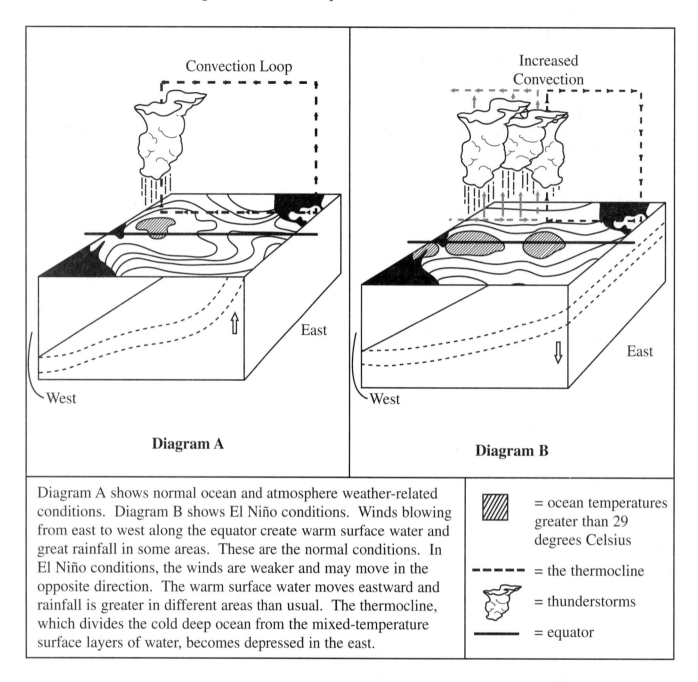

Diagram A shows normal ocean and atmosphere weather-related conditions. Diagram B shows El Niño conditions. Winds blowing from east to west along the equator create warm surface water and great rainfall in some areas. These are the normal conditions. In El Niño conditions, the winds are weaker and may move in the opposite direction. The warm surface water moves eastward and rainfall is greater in different areas than usual. The thermocline, which divides the cold deep ocean from the mixed-temperature surface layers of water, becomes depressed in the east.

= ocean temperatures greater than 29 degrees Celsius

= the thermocline

= thunderstorms

= equator

1. Name three changes that occur under El Niño conditions.

2. How can El Niño research (like the kind that created these diagrams) make a difference for people around the world? Can learning how El Niño works help people in some way?

Sweden's Igloo Inn

Sometimes on a very chilly night, the cold creeps in. It creeps beneath the thickest blankets. It creeps through the warmest pajamas and inside the coziest socks. Brrrr! It finds a set of toes to nip.

At the Ice Hotel in Sweden, the cold doesn't have to sneak in. Guests expect the cold to nip at their toes. And their fingers. And their noses. That's because the entire hotel is made of ice and snow. Even the furniture is made of ice.

Why would anyone spend money to stay in a snow fort? Its beauty attracts many guests. Guests who survive the low temperatures receive a printed Ice Hotel Certificate to prove they have beaten the cold. The manager says, "After they spend the night, in the morning they feel like Tarzan or He-Man because they slept in there."

For eight years, a shiny new Ice Hotel has been built from fresh ice and snow each winter. Last year about 4,000 people checked in for a night at the Ice Hotel. Guest pay an $80 room charge. They get extra warm snowsuits and mummy-style sleeping bags. Guests need all the extra padding they can get. The hotel's "beds" are actually ice blocks covered with reindeer skins! One hotel visitor said she had started to have second thoughts about spending the night there. "It's freezing!" she said. "Apparently everybody makes out O.K. But after I saw the beds, I got a little worried."

By May, warmer temperatures will melt the hotel. But it's not gone for good. Builders start chipping away at another Ice Hotel in October.

Sweden's Igloo Inn (cont.)

Directions: Answer these questions. You may look at the story.

1. Where is the hotel?

2. What is unique about the hotel?

3. What does a person receive for staying at the hotel?

4. What do guests receive to help them stay warm?

5. Draw a picture or write a detailed description of how you think the ice hotel looks.

6. Why do you think a person would want to stay at the hotel?

7. What do you think would be the best part about staying at an ice hotel?

8. Do you think the guests get to have heaters in their rooms? Explain why or why not.

9. Compose a fictional letter to a friend telling about your experience staying at the ice hotel.

Sweden's Igloo Inn *(cont.)*

Directions: Look at the chart. Answer the questions.

Degrees Celsius (°C)	Condition
0	freezing point of water (ice)
20 to 25	average room temperature
37	average human body temperature
100	boiling point of water

1. Using the chart and what you already know about ice, what do you think a person would need for a comfortable stay at the Ice Hotel?

2. Could a person always live in a place made of ice? Explain why you do or do not think so. Use the chart to support your answer.

Note: Need help remembering what Celsius temperatures mean? Try remembering this rhyme about Celsius:

    30 is hot.

    20 is nice.

    10 is cold.

    Zero is ice!

Directions: Read the story.

Back to the Moon!

A half-moon was shining. The rocket's engines began to roar. People on the ground cheered as it blasted off from Cape Canaveral. "We're on our way!" said scientist Scott Hubbard.

A small spacecraft was tucked inside the rocket's nose. It was called *Lunar Prospector.* An hour after takeoff, the spacecraft broke free. It began a 4 1/2-day trip to the moon.

The last time NASA sent a mission to the moon was in 1972. "It certainly feels good to be going back," said scientist Joseph Boyce.

There are no astronauts on board *Prospector.* It will not land on the moon. Prospector will spend a year traveling around the moon.

Prospector will help answer questions about the moon. How did the moon form? What is it made of? Could humans live there someday?

In 1963, NASA created the Apollo space program to explore the moon. The most exciting moment came in 1969. That's when astronauts landed on the moon. They did experiments and collected rocks. But Apollo left many questions unanswered.

Prospector has tools to map the moon's surface. Other tools will study what the moon is made of.

A water supply on the moon could make it possible for people to live there. An air supply would also be needed. With the right equipment, people can live in strange places. "We have a year-round base in Antarctica," says Boyce. "Today's kids may end up living on the moon."

Back to the Moon! *(cont.)*

Directions: Answer these questions. You may look at the story.

1. What is the name of the spacecraft?

2. Where did the spacecraft travel?

3. What is the purpose of *Prospector*?

4. What happened in 1969?

5. Imagine that you were able to live on the moon. Write a paragraph describing what your life would be like.

6. What do you think is the importance of studying the moon?

7. Why would scientists want to find a water supply on the moon?

8. Describe what you think it would be like to be at Cape Canaveral watching a rocket launch.

Back to the Moon! *(cont.)*

Directions: Look at the outline. Answer the questions.

Back-to-the-Moon Outline

   I. *Lunar Prospector* was launched.

       A. It would spend $4\frac{1}{2}$ days flying to the moon.

  II. *Prospector* will travel around the moon for a year.

       A. It will answer questions about the moon.

          1. From what is it made?

          2. How was it formed?

          3. Could humans live there someday?

 III. *Prospector* has many tools on board.

       A. Some tools will study the moon's surface.

       B. Some tools will study what makes up the moon.

---

1. Compare the outline to the article. What facts from the article are not mentioned on the outline?

2. How is an outline helpful to use for writing?

A New Viking Voyage

In August 1998, a wooden ship set sail along Greenland's west coast. Writer and explorer W. Hodding Carter was onboard. From the time he was 10, he has dreamed about the Vikings. "I was always reading history books and imagining I was a Viking," he said.

Carter, 35, decided to make his dream come true. He asked a man named Robert Stevens to build a knarr. This is a Viking merchant ship with oars and a square sail. Carter, Stevens, and eight others sailed the path of Viking Leif Eriksson.

Eriksson came to North America 1,000 years ago. This was about 500 years before Columbus.

The voyage was the second try for Carter's crew. In July 1997, they had to stop when the boat's rudder broke. The crew members couldn't steer without a rudder. They started this trip in Nuuk where the last trip ended. They had a new rudder. Carter was even wearing Viking clothes!

Vikings didn't have good tools to judge direction or distance. They found their way by spotting landmarks. They watched for birds. This was a sign that land was near. At night, they steered by the North Star. Vikings believed the earth was flat. Still, they sailed bravely into the unknown.

Carter's crew tried to sail the way Vikings did. But they had modern compasses and a lifeboat. They also had a medical kit in case of an emergency. Like the Vikings, they didn't know what adventures awaited them on their journey.

A New Viking Voyage (cont.)

Directions: Answer these questions. You may look at the story.

1. About what did Carter dream?

2. What did he have built?

3. How was Carter planning to make his dream come true?

4. How many attempts did Carter make?

5. Make a list comparing the similarities and differences between Carter's voyage and Eriksson's voyage 1,000 years ago.

6. What did Vikings steer by at night?

7. Why do you think Carter brought modern compasses, a lifeboat, and an emergency kit on his voyage?

8. Why is the sight of birds a sign that land is near?

9. What do you think would be the most dangerous thing about a voyage of this kind?

A New Viking Voyage (cont.)

Directions: Look at the map. Answer the questions.

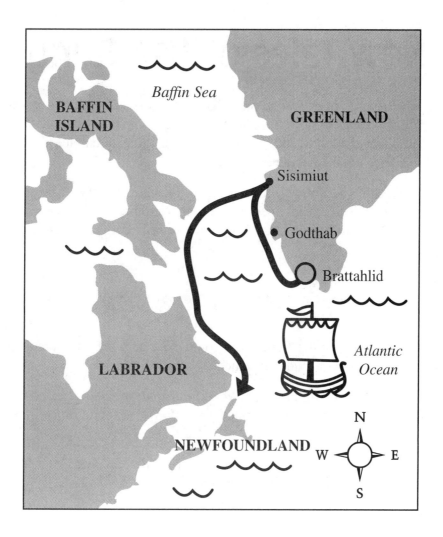

1. What is the purpose of this map?

2. In what direction did the crew first sail?

3. Why did the crew follow this route?

Directions: Read the story.

New Tales of the Taino

Sometimes the best treasures are the ones that tell a story. Deep in the forest of the Dominican Republic is a watery hole filled with treasures. The hole contains more than 240 objects. There are chairs, jars, baskets, and bowls. These things are at least 500 years old. They belonged to a tribe called the Taino.

Until now, very little was known about them. But each object that is pulled from the well tells about who they were. These people lived in areas that are now called Cuba, Puerto Rico, Haiti, and the Dominican Republic. They grew squash, corn, and beans. They built canoes. They fished.

But in 1492, their lives changed forever. That is when Columbus and other explorers came. The explorers took the Taino's land. They spread new diseases. They killed many people. The Taino did not fight back.

By the 1520s, nearly all of the Taino were gone. All that were left were a few of their words, including hurricane, barbecue, and canoe.

The people used wood to build things. Wood falls apart over long periods of time. That is what makes the well so amazing. One scientist says, "We've found more Taino remains at this one site than ever before."

Another rich Taino site has been found on the north side of Cuba. After 500 years, it seems that the story of the Taino will finally be told.

New Tales of the Taino *(cont.)*

Directions: Answer these questions. You may look at the story.

1. In what country were the treasures found?

2. How old are the items that were found?

3. Why do you think so little was known about the people?

4. What changed the lives of the Taino forever?

5. What are three ways that explorers hurt the people?

6. Write a story about a "treasure" that you own.

7. Explain the viewpoints of the Taino and of the explorers. How do you think each felt about the explorers arriving?

8. Describe the importance of finding the Taino treasures.

9. What do you think would have happened if the Taino had decided to fight back?

New Tales of the Taino (cont.)

Directions: Look at the map. Answer the questions.

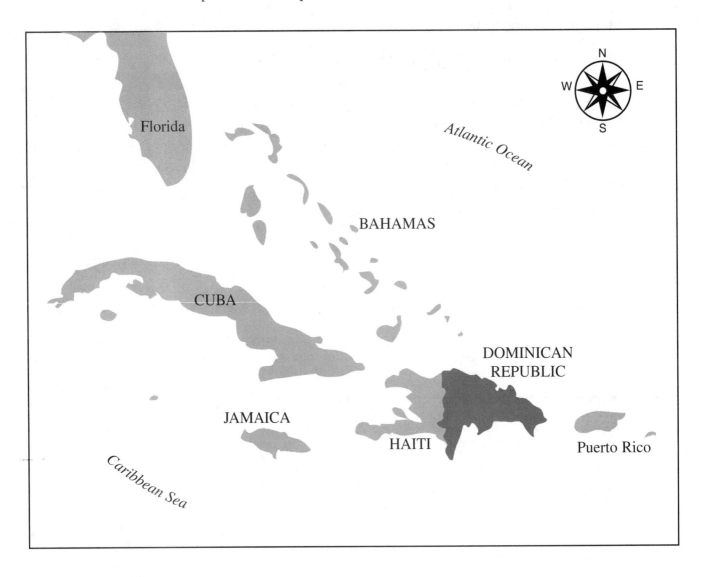

1. What state in the United States is closest to the Dominican Republic?

2. Why do you think that some of our English words (hurricane, barbecue, and canoe) came from the Taino people?

John Glenn

In 1962, John Glenn traveled around the earth. He was all by himself. The spacecraft was called *Friendship 7*. It was less than 10 feet long. At age 40, he was proud to be the first American to do this. After his career as an astronaut, Glenn became a U.S. senator. Then, in October 1998, Glenn returned to space. He was 77 years old. He served as part of a crew in the space shuttle *Discovery*. The leader of the shuttle was 42 years old. The trip was a success. Glenn and the rest of the crew returned safely. Glenn's flight helped scientists study the effects of aging. It captured the interest of Americans. It made them think twice about doubting the capabilities of older Americans.

John Glenn (cont.)

Directions: Answer these questions. You may look at the story.

1. What did Glenn do in 1962?

2. Who was with him on *Friendship 7*?

3. How did Glenn's second flight help scientists?

4. Why do you think it is so exciting that Glenn returned to space?

5. Write a list of similarities and differences between Glenn's two trips in space.

6. Imagine that you are an old man or woman. What kinds of things do you hope to be able to do at that age?

7. Explain what you think is the importance of studying aging.

8. Write a summary of the article using only three sentences.

John Glenn (cont.)

Directions: Look at the chart. Answer the questions.

		1962	1998
The Astronaut	Height	5 feet 10 inches	5 feet 10 inches
	Hair color	red	white
	Age	40	77
The Spacecraft	Name	*Friendship 7*	*Discovery*
	Crew size	1	7
	Windows	1	10
	Computers	0	5

1. What two differences are shown about John Glenn between the two space journeys?

2. By looking at the chart, what can you tell about the difference in size between the two spacecrafts?

3. What does the chart indicate about the difference in technology between 1962 and 1998?

Directions: Read the story.

A Land of Their Own

It was midnight on April 1, 1999. Fireworks lit up the sky over the village of Iqaluit. Canada had a new territory. It is called Nunavut. The name means "our land" in their language.

Nunavut is a large area. It is made of tundra, islands, and lakes. The icy land reaches to the top of the world. It includes the north magnetic pole. Not many people live there. There are 28 villages. The largest village has just 4,000 people.

This land is now on the maps. It is the first time the map of Canada has been changed in 50 years. For the first time in Canada, native people control their own government. Inuit make up 85% of the population. On February 15, the people held their first election. Fifteen of the 18 members of the new law makers are Inuit. Inuktitut is the language they use. French and English are also spoken. Inuit now control education, health and social services in the area.

"All our powers were taken away by the white man," says a lawmaker. "Now we're finally taking them back."

A Land of Their Own (cont.)

Directions: Answer these questions. You may look at the story.

1. What was celebrated on April 1, 1999?

2. What is the name of the territory?

3. What does the name mean?

4. What is the land made up of?

5. Draw a picture of how you think the territory looks?

6. Why do you think the new territory is important to the native people?

7. Imagine that you are a newspaper reporter in Canada. Write a short article about the new territory and its importance.

8. Why do you think it is important for the native people to control their own education, health, and social services?

9. What does it mean that their powers were taken away by the white man?

A Land of Their Own *(cont.)*

Directions: Look at the map. Answer the questions.

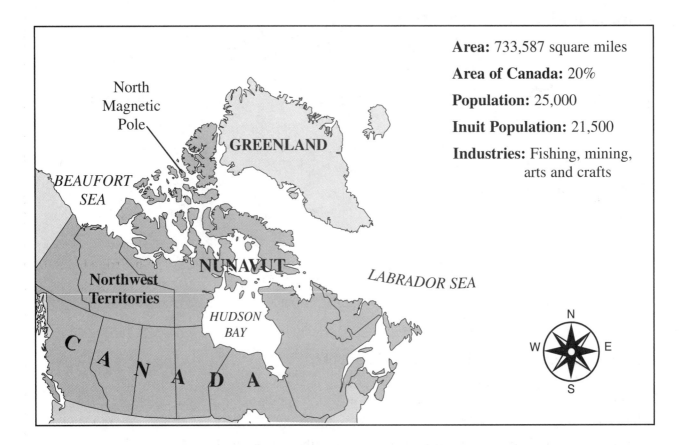

Numbers on Nunavut		
Category	**Number**	**Note**
People per square mile of land	1/30	That's 1 person per 30 square miles!
Roads	1	It is 13 miles long.
Caribou per person	30	Reindeer outnumber people 30 to 1.
Months of winter	9	Three-fourths of every year is winter.

1. What information do the map and chart give that the article did not?

2. If there is only one road in Nunavut, how do you think people travel?

Directions: Read the story.

Frozen in Time

The Andes Mountains are in Peru. Researchers made a discovery there. They found a mummy of a 12-year-old girl. They call her Juanita.

The girl was an Inca. The Incas ruled part of South America. They were there before the Spaniards arrived to conquer the territory.

Juanita's body was frozen. Because of this she is well preserved. Scientists say we will be able to learn a lot from her. They can learn about the health of Inca's by studying her organs.

Johan Reinhard is an American anthropologist. He found Juanita. He and his friend worked hard to get the mummy down the icy slope. They found two more mummies, too.

They also found statues. These were made of gold, silver, and shell. Clothing and feather headdresses on the statues had been perfectly preserved. When Reinhard saw them, he said, "Holy smokes! The statues are just sticking out of the ground."

The three mummies may have been sacrificed. This means they were killed in a religious ceremony. The Incas believed that mountain gods caused natural disasters. They thought the gods would stop disasters if they sacrificed people. People chosen to be killed saw it as a great honor.

A force of nature uncovered the treasures. A volcano erupted. It caused the ice to melt. This exposed the statues and mummies. Scientists think that was a lucky accident. The Incas might have said the gods finally decided to show the world more of the amazing Inca culture.

Frozen in Time *(cont.)*

Directions: Answer these questions. You may look at the story.

1. In what country did researchers make their discovery?

2. What did they find?

3. Why was Juanita's body so well preserved?

4. What can be learned from her body?

5. Explain why the Incas sacrificed people.

6. Why do you think people thought it was an honor to be sacrificed?

7. Describe what happened that uncovered the treasures.

8. Draw a picture of what Reinhard might have seen when he discovered the site.

Frozen in Time *(cont.)*

Directions: Look at the map. Answer the questions.

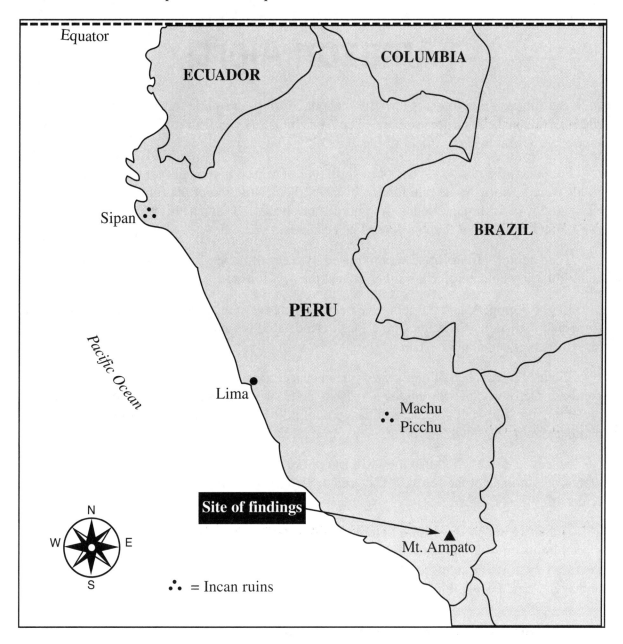

1. In what part of Peru were the treasures found (northern, southern, eastern, western)?

2. Mt. Ampato is not far from the equator. Why do you think the area was icy?

Directions: Read the story.

Amazon Alert!

The Amazon rain forest is lush. It is about 2.7 million square miles. Parrots, jaguars, and piranhas make their homes there. The Amazon holds one-fifth of the world's freshwater supply. It has the widest variety of life.

For years, the rain forest has been shrinking. Farmers and others clear the land. The 1990s were terrible for the rain forest. In 1995, the destruction of the forest was worse than ever. About 11,200 square miles were burned or cleared. That's nearly twice what was lost in 1994. One-eighth of the rain forest has been destroyed.

The bad news from Brazil was followed by a ray of hope. Brazil promised to do a better job. It would enforce laws that protect the rain forest.

Loggers, miners, and farmers have been moving into the Amazon. Some cut down trees for wood. Others burn the forest to clear the land. Roads have also damaged the area. The loss of trees is called deforestation.

Pictures were taken of the Amazon from space. Brazil based its information on these pictures. Deforestation slowed down in 1996 and 1997. That's not because people were protecting the forest. It's because of heavy rainfall. It made it harder to burn trees. "These numbers are no reason to celebrate," says Brazil's Environment Minister.

Scientists are worried that they will run out of time. They won't be able to study the plants and animals of the forest. "The great tragedy is how much isn't known," says one scientist.

Brazil wanted to slow down deforestation. It decided to get tough. In 1996, Brazil placed limits on clearing land. But the laws were not always enforced. Now those who hurt the rain forest will be punished. They will get big fines. They will also be ordered to fix the damage. Some people think there is still hope.

Amazon Alert! *(cont.)*

Directions: Answer these questions. You may look at the story.

1. Why has the rain forest been shrinking?

2. How many square miles of rain forest land was burned or cleared in 1995?

3. What did Brazil promise to do?

4. Create a plan for how you would work to protect the rain forest.

5. Loggers, miners, and farmers earn a living from the rain forest. What would you recommend that they do to earn money instead?

6. Define deforestation.

7. Why did deforestation slow down in 1996 and 1997?

8. Explain why it is important to protect the rain forest.

9. People who hurt the rain forest will have to fix the damage. Explain how a person might fix the damage done by burning or clear cutting.

Amazon Alert! *(cont.)*

Directions: Look at the graph. Answer the questions.

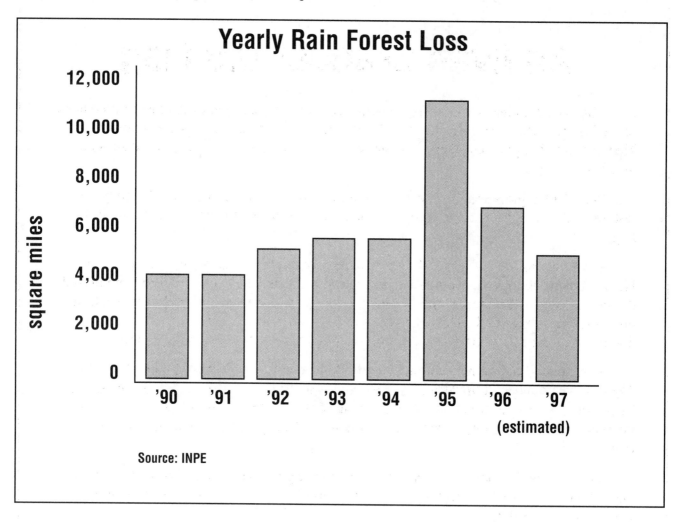

Yearly Rain Forest Loss

Source: INPE

1. Compare the loss of rain forest from 1995 to 1997. What happened?

2. How does this graph help you to better understand the article?

3. What do you think the graph would show for 1998? Why?

An Even Grander Old Flag

"Oh, say, does that star-spangled banner yet wave/O'er the land of the free and the home of the brave?" Those words are part of the U.S. national anthem. They were written in 1814. They haven't changed since then. But the flag has changed a lot. Its stripes and stars are faded and worn.

Some of the glory will be returned to the flag. A three-year project of $5.5 million will restore it. A young lawyer named Francis Scott Key wrote those words after seeing of the flag.

It was during the War of 1812. Key was at Fort McHenry near Baltimore, Maryland. He saw a British attack on the American Army. He watched as cannons boomed and blazed through the night. The next morning, he wasn't sure who had won. Then, he looked through his telescope. He spotted something. It was a huge American flag waving from the fort. The sight inspired Key. He quickly wrote the words to "The Star-Spangled Banner."

It can be seen at the National Museum of American History in Washington, D.C. The flag is 150 pounds of cloth. Since that time, light, pollution and moist air have damaged it. Visitors will be able to watch as the flag is cleaned and treated. This will prevent it from more damage. The History Channel is helping to fund the project. It will air a special on the flag.

The flag's flying days are over. Even still, the original star-spangled banner still inspires many Americans. Libby O'Connell says, "It is part of our heritage and part of a really wonderful history story."

An Even Grander Old Flag (cont.)

Directions: Answer these questions. You may look at the story.

1. What is the name of the song quoted at the beginning of the article?

2. Who wrote the U.S. national anthem?

3. What inspired him to write the song?

4. What has damaged the old flag?

5. Write what the American flag represents to you.

6. Why do you think it is important to people that the flag is repaired?

7. Draw a picture of the American flag.

8. Rewrite the third paragraph of the article.

An Even Grander Old Flag *(cont.)*

Directions: Look at the flags. Answer the questions.

The American flag has changed throughout the years. Below you can see three American flags.

Betsy Ross Flag

The 21 Star Flag

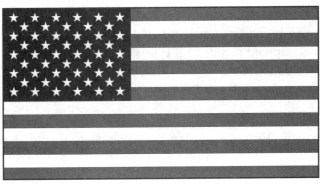

50 Star Flag

1. Why do you think the American flag has changed over the years?

2. What do the stars on the flag represent?

3. How would our flag change if there was a new state added to the United States?

Lighting Up the Night Sky

Something very strange happened in November 1833. For two nights, people across the U.S. stood in their yards and pointed to the sky. They couldn't believe their eyes! Thousands of fast-moving fireballs streaked across the heavens. Clouds of smoke twisted like snakes and hung in the air behind the fireballs. No one knew what was happening. Some people took cover. They were afraid that stars were falling out of the sky. Others held up their hands. They were hoping to catch one of the flying lights.

The people were seeing a meteor storm. Very little was known about meteors in 1833. Today scientists can tell us what causes them. They can even predict when other meteor showers will occur. In fact, they think the same storm from 1833 will return!

Meteor showers can occur when a comet passes close to the earth. In November 1998, a comet named Tempel-Tuttle was nearby. This comet orbits the sun every 33 years. Like all other comets, this one is a big, dirty space snowball. It is made of ice and rock. As a comet gets near the sun, it heats up and pieces of it come off. These pieces are not larger than grains of sand. They are called meteoroids. They trail the comet until they enter the earth's atmosphere. Then they explode. The burning meteoroids are called meteors.

A meteor storm takes place when lots of meteors burn up at once. This happens only when a comet comes close. Even then, scientists can't be sure how heavy a meteor storm will be. One scientist says, "All you can do is make an educated guess."

The meteoroids that trail Tempel-Tuttle have a name. They are called Leonids. They are named after Leo, the group of stars that they appear to come from. The storm was back in 1999 because the comet was still near Earth. Now it will be a long wait!

Lighting Up the Night Sky (cont.)

Directions: Answer these questions. You may look at the story.

1. What did people see in November 1833?

2. How did people feel about what they saw?

3. What causes a meteor shower?

4. Imagine that you lived in 1833. Write a letter to the people explaining what they saw in the sky and why they shouldn't be afraid.

5. How many years separated the meteor shower in 1833 and the one in 1999?

6. Explain the steps in forming meteoroids.

7. Why do you think scientists are interested in studying meteors?

8. Summarize the article using five sentences or less.

Lighting Up the Night Sky *(cont.)*

Directions: Look at the information chart. Answer the questions.

Did You Know?

- Meteoroids can hurtle through space at 160,000 miles an hour!

- At that speed, even a tiny speck could damage a spacecraft or satellite. To prepare for the Leonids, scientists turn spacecraft so their strongest sides face the meteoroids.

- Meteor showers are less dramatic than meteor storms, but easier to catch. The Perseids put on a show every August.

- Meteors are also called shooting stars, but they aren't stars at all.

---

1. How does this chart add to the article?

2. What fact on the chart do you think is most interesting?

3. Why do you think that people call meteors shooting stars?

Directions: Read the story.

See Africa by Bike

You are invited to set out on an amazing journey. It is across East Africa. You will trek through thick jungles. You will ride through hot deserts. You will cross the Serengeti Plain. Lions, elephants, and zebras roam there. You will climb snowy Mount Kilimanjaro. That is the highest peak in Africa. Along the way you will meet scientists and animal experts. You may even have the chance to form answers to problems hurting Africa's environment.

Joining you will be Dan Buettner. He is the leader of the trip. His team will make the trip on mountain bikes. It will last six weeks and cover 1,500 miles. Their packs will weigh 100 pounds. They will be loaded with laptop computers and supplies. They will ride 60 miles a day and camp out at night. Your trail plans are easy. You will tag along on the Internet.

Buettner has set three world records for bicycling. "Bicycle travel is the greatest teacher of all," he says. Six years ago, he began to work with scientists. His travels are available to kids on the Internet. Each trip can be followed at his Web site. For a fee, a class can take a more active role. They can e-mail the group and ask questions. They can even vote for what route the team should take.

Buettner led an exploration in Central America. They went to a Mayan civilization. Kids helped scientists figure out the population of an ancient city. Buettner tells young explorers, "Your ideas count and may lead to some great discoveries!"

See Africa by Bike (cont.)

Directions: Answer these questions. You may look at the story.

1. Where are you invited to go?

2. How are you able to go on this trip?

3. Who is Dan Buettner?

4. The trip will last six weeks and cover 1,500 miles. How many miles a week would they travel?

5. If a class pays a fee, what can they do on the Web site?

6. If you could go on an adventure, where would you go and how would you travel?

7. What problems do you think are hurting Africa's land and wildlife?

8. Why did Buettner say that kids' ideas count?

9. Imagine that you are on the trip in Africa. Write a letter telling about what you have seen and done.

See Africa by Bike (cont.)

Directions: Look at the diagram. Answer the questions.

Mount Kilimanjaro actually has several cones that are volcanoes. These volcanoes have not been active in modern times, but sometimes they emit gases and steam.

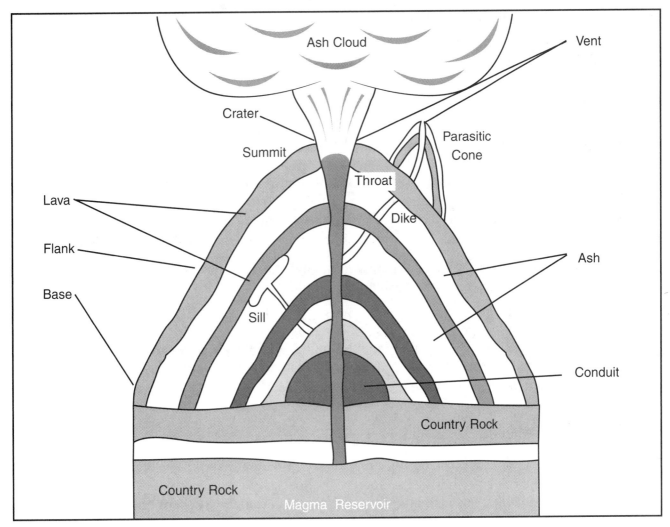

Parts of a Volcano

1. How does magma get from the magma reservoir to a parasitic cone?

2. Why do you think a part of the volcano is called a "throat"?

3. If Mount Kilimanjaro is not an active volcano, why do you think it emits steam from time to time?

Saving the Swordfish

Americans are hooked on swordfish. But this dish will no longer be served at some restaurants. Swordfish numbers are shrinking fast. There are 27 U.S. chefs who want people to notice the problem. They are taking swordfish off their menus for at least a year.

Until the 1950s, fishermen caught these fish by harpoon. These are large fish. They weigh 200 to 1,200 pounds. They were easy targets and ended up on dinner plates. Small fish were left in the sea. They could grow and reproduce.

During the 1960s, fishermen began using long lines. They had hundreds of hooks. These lines could trap many more swordfish. They catch small fish. They also catch females who have not yet given birth. The result? Swordfish numbers have dropped by more than half.

Many nations have set limits. Fishermen can only take a certain amount. But this has not stopped some. They reel in more than their limit.

The limits are "too little too late," says Carl Safina. He favors a return to harpooning.

Environmentalists and restaurants teamed up in 1998. They want to allow swordfish to make a comeback. Meanwhile, the United Nations battled overfishing. They named 1998 the International Year of the Ocean.

"We depend on the supply of fish and have a responsibility to ensure that it continues," says chef Rick Moonen. He won't serve swordfish. He hopes to teach diners about this.

But a swordfish comeback depends on the help of more restaurants. Not everyone is ready to let the catch go. The large seafood chain Red Lobster has no plans to stop serving swordfish. And some chefs claim the swordfish boycott is unfair to fishermen.

Increasing swordfish numbers could take up to 10 years. That's even if many restaurants join in. Lisa Speer says, "We just want to give the fish a break, so that future generations can enjoy them."

Saving the Swordfish (cont.)

Directions: Answer these questions. You may look at the story.

1. Why won't swordfish be served in many restaurants?

2. What is the problem that swordfish face?

3. Even though limits have been set, what is still happening?

4. Create a campaign to get more restaurants to stop serving swordfish.

5. Write a letter to a restaurant such as Red Lobster explaining why swordfish need our help.

6. Why is it bad when female swordfish are caught?

7. Explain the difference between the methods of catching swordfish in the 1950s and now.

8. What do you think will happen if large numbers of swordfish continue to be caught and sold?

Saving the Swordfish *(cont.)*

Directions: Look at the graph. Answer the questions.

Swordfish aren't the only fish vanishing. Overfishing could wipe out many species, from orange roughy to bluefin tuna. The amount of fish caught in the world's oceans jumped from some 20 million tons in 1950 to 90 million in 1995.

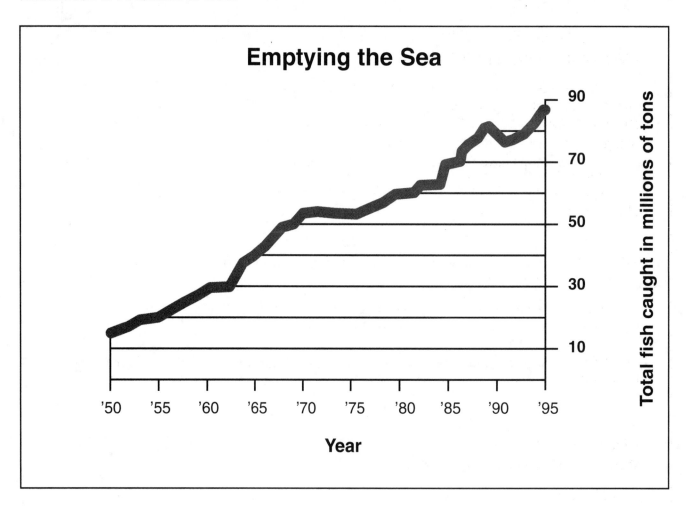

1. Why do you think this graph is called Emptying the Sea?

2. What does this graph show you about the number of fish that are caught?

3. How could you use this graph to make people aware of the swordfish problem?

The School Is One Big Bird Feeder!

"This is our tree!" shout the fourth-graders. The three friends sling their arms across one another's shoulders. They rejoice at the sight of their newly planted tree.

Why all the excitement over a skinny sapling? Because there's not much that's green and growing in the neighborhood where the boys attend school. Grass in this section of Knoxville, Tennessee, is mostly dead and brown. Dull, brown buildings tower in places where green trees and shrubs used to grow.

But thanks to 17 fourth-graders at Beaumont Elementary Honors Academy, green is making a comeback. Guided by their teacher, students have planted 19 trees. They have planted ginkgoes, birches, and maples.

The new trees do more than add color. They are also part of a plan hatched by the class. They want to attract birds to the area. Birds are an "indicator species." That means that when they are living in an area, other animals will follow.

The plan began when students began asking for donations for trees. They wrote letters and hung posters. It wasn't long before money began to arrive.

Next, each student "adopted" a different type of bird native to the area. Then students lured local birds with a treat. They used pinecones smeared with peanut butter and birdseed.

It worked! Birds started arriving the next day. But those sticky pinecones were just the beginning. The class soon began building more bird feeders. They made the feeders out of lumber scraps. "I've learned a lot about being a volunteer," says Carlyn Grieve. "It helps show that everyone can work together."

The teamwork of the class has not gone unnoticed. The city of Knoxville decided to give $3,000 to the school. The school plans to use the money to build a nature trail. They also want to build a pond. This would bring in even more birds and other wildlife to the area. With the green team on the case, brown seems to be an endangered color in Knoxville.

The School Is One Big Bird Feeder! (cont.)

Directions: Answer these questions. You may look at the story.

1. Why did the class decide to plant trees?

2. What did they hope the trees would bring?

3. What is an "indicator species"?

4. If you wanted to raise money for a community project, how would you do it?

5. Draw a picture of a bird feeder that you could make.

6. Make a list of supplies you would need in order to make a bird feeder.

7. Write a letter to your teacher or principal about the importance of trees and birds to your community.

8. Why do you think the author calls the class "the green team"?

9. Why did the author say that "brown seems to be an endangered color"?

The School Is One Big Bird Feeder! *(cont.)*

Directions: Use information from the article to add two subtopics to each topic on the idea web below.

Idea Web

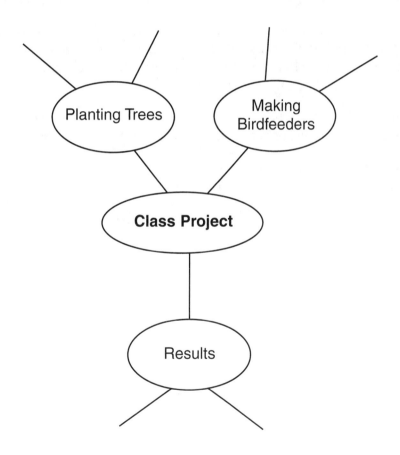

A War Against Land Mines

Jody Williams greeted reporters. She was barefoot and wearing blue jeans. She is the world's new Number One peacemaker. She had just received a special present. On October 1, 1997, Williams was given one of the world's best honors. She won a Nobel Peace Prize. She received a $1 million award. It was for her work to rid the world of land mines. These are deadly underground explosives.

The prize is named after Alfred Nobel, who invented dynamite in the 1800s. Nobel did not want to be remembered only for creating something destructive. So he left his money to reward people. The rewards go to those who work for the "good of humanity." People are awarded for work in sciences and literature. The awards are also for economics and peace.

Williams shares the prize with her organization. It is called the International Campaign to Ban Land Mines. In just six years, Williams has helped urge some 100 countries to stop using the deadly weapons. More than 26,000 people are killed or hurt by land mines each year. Many of them are children.

In December, a treaty will be signed. It is calling for a ban on land mines. More than 100 nations plan to sign. But some big nations won't sign! One of those is the U.S.

President Clinton says he doesn't want a ban on land mines. He wants the U.S. to be able to use them in unsafe areas where soldiers are.

Williams vows to keep up her fight. She wants to get rid of all land mines.

A War Against Land Mines (cont.)

Directions: Answer these questions. You may look at the story.

1. What is Jody Williams famous for?

2. What is a land mine?

3. For what purpose is the Nobel Peace Prize awarded?

4. How many people are killed or hurt by land mines each year?

5. If land mines are buried under the ground, how do you think they can be found in order to remove them?

6. Why do you think that land mines are used?

7. Write a letter to the president about ridding the world of land mines. Provide facts to support your opinion.

8. Write a summary of the work Jody Williams does.

A War Against Land Mines *(cont.)*

Directions: Look at the map. Answer the questions.

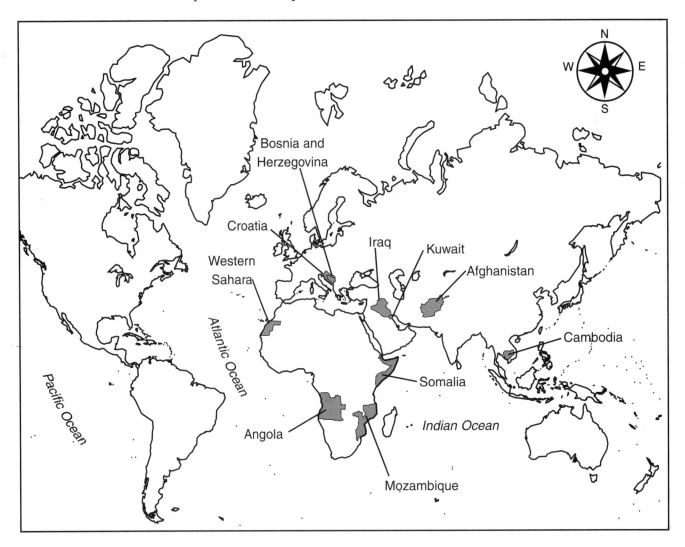

1. Why is this map called Danger Zones?

2. What does the map show?

3. Compare the number of land mines in Africa to the U.S.

Directions: Read the story.

A Picture-Perfect Job

Just call him "Sure-Shot Schick." Ryan Schick is 15 years old. He's a photographer. He landed a job most professional photographers would love. He took photos at the World Series!

Ryan got his start when he was 10. That's when he met Steve Liss, a professional photographer. They were at a rally in Lee's Summit, Missouri. Ryan got Liss's address and wrote to him. Liss says, "I knew after the third letter that this kid was serious." He decided to show Ryan the ropes.

The two went to Little Rock, Arkansas, after Bill Clinton was elected president. Ryan videotaped the victory speech. "Clinton knelt down and saluted me," he says. *TIME* magazine published Ryan's first photo when he was 13. It shows police dragging a man away from a political rally.

Ryan was at the World Series as Liss's backup photographer. Ryan's dream photo of the Series was a long shot. "I wanted to shoot a World Series ball coming at me and breaking my camera, without hurting the film," he says. He had to settle for action shots on the field.

Now Ryan's focus is back on school. In the future, he hopes to find full-time work taking pictures.

A Picture-Perfect Job (cont.)

Directions: Answer these questions. You may look at the story.

1. What is Ryan's job?

2. What big assignment did he get?

3. How old is Ryan?

4. Why is it amazing that Ryan is a photographer?

5. Ryan has a job that is usually only held by adults. What adult job would you like to do now?

6. What do you think it takes in order to be a good photographer?

7. Explain the shot that Ryan wanted to get at the World Series. Was he successful?

8. Think about the ideal job that you would like to have. What training or education will you need in order to perform this job?

A Picture-Perfect Job *(cont.)*

Directions: Look at the diagram. Answer the questions.

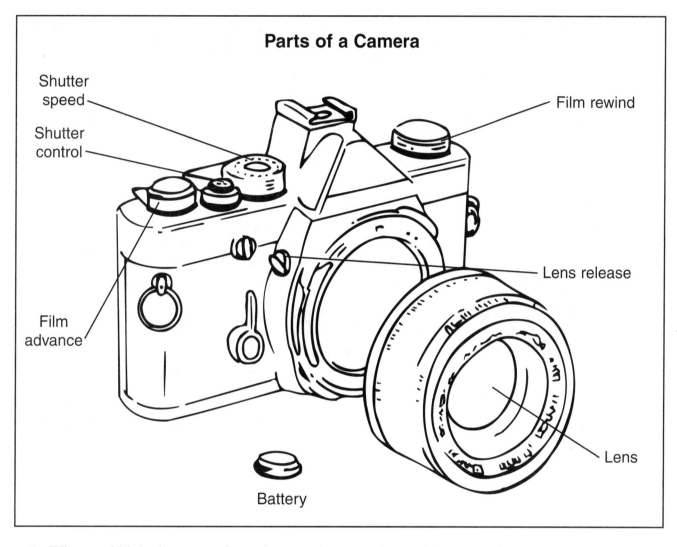

Parts of a Camera

Shutter speed

Shutter control

Film advance

Film rewind

Lens release

Lens

Battery

1. Why would it be important for a photographer to understand the parts of his or her camera?

2. What do you think the shutter is on a camera?

3. Ryan is a very experienced photographer. What does this illustration tell you about his knowledge of cameras?

Directions: Read the story.

The Perils of Peanuts

At first, you feel an itchy throat and runny nose. Next, you feel like throwing up. Then, you can't even breathe. That is an allergic reaction. It's what it can happen to a person who is allergic to peanuts. Without the proper medicine, the person might die. Some people are really allergic. They will have this kind of reaction after smelling or touching anything that has peanut oil or dust.

Many people are allergic to peanuts. They are the most common food to which people are allergic. Now they are under attack. Airlines and restaurants have to make changes. They are being asked to stop serving them. Then people won't risk being near peanut bits or dust. In some schools, cafeterias are setting aside peanut-free tables. Other schools are putting a full ban on peanut-butter products. That includes peanut-butter sandwiches.

But will a peanut ban ensure that no one will be exposed to peanuts? Some foods may have peanut oil in them. People don't even know it. Peanut defenders say allergic people should use careful food habits. They should also wash their hands to protect themselves.

The Perils of Peanuts *(cont.)*

Directions: Answer these questions. You may look at the story.

1. What are some symptoms of allergic reactions?

2. If not given medicine, what can happen to a person with a reaction to peanuts?

3. How are restaurants and airlines changing? Why?

4. If a person allergic to peanuts can react to smelling or touching peanuts, in what ways and in what situations would he or she need to be careful?

5. In a cafeteria, what is a peanut-free table?

6. What does it mean if a school puts a "full ban on peanut-butter products"?

7. How can a person be exposed to peanuts or peanut oil without knowing it?

8. What precautions would a person have to take if he or she had an allergy to peanuts?

9. Design a poster that could be posted near a peanut-free table in a cafeteria.

The Perils of Peanuts (cont.)

Directions: Look at the fact sheet. Answer the questions.

What Is an Allergy?

One in 20 kids has a food allergy. The most common food that people are allergic to is peanuts, followed by all kinds of nuts, fish, shellfish (such as shrimp and crab), milk, eggs, wheat, and soy.

Besides food, people can be allergic to dust, pollen from plants, and many other things. When an allergic person eats or breathes in one of these substances, the body thinks it is a harmful invader and tries to attack it. The body's tiny attackers, called histamines, are released into the blood. This causes the blood vessels to get bigger and the skin to swell and itch. It also triggers the nose, throat, and lungs to produce sticky mucus. In many cases, a medicine called an antihistamine (Get it?) can relieve these symptoms.

---

1. Based on the information above, what dangers could an allergic person face at school?

2. What, specifically, do you think an antihistamine does?

3. Plan a school lunch menu that would likely not cause any person with allergies to have an attack.

He's Young and Wired

The Minister of Technology in Jamaica is Philip Paulwell. He is the head of high technology (high tech). But last year the nation's official Web site needed changing. No one knew how to do it.

He turned to a 13-year-old named Makonnen. He was visiting the office with his mother. He was able to upload new information for the Web site. Paulwell was very impressed. He gave the boy a job. Makonnen helps find ways to bring high-tech education to Jamaica. He also finds ways to bring in high-tech jobs.

Once a week he reports to his boss. He tells him about the latest high-tech news. He also shares ideas for teaching Jamaicans to be more computer-smart.

The teen began using his mother's computer when he was young. "I'd press a button to see what would happen," he says. "Then when I'd mess something up on the computer, I had to learn to fix it."

He is Jamaica's youngest government adviser. The young man takes his job seriously, but he still likes to play computer games. When he is older, he hopes to design his own games. "I have many goals," says the computer whiz. "I would like to change the world—especially Jamaica."

He's Young and Wired (cont.)

Directions: Answer these questions. You may look at the story.

1. What was Makonnen able to do for Philip Paulwell?

2. Why was this amazing?

3. What is Makonnen's job?

4. What kinds of things do you know how to do on the computer?

5. Why do you think it is important for Jamaica to have high-tech education for students?

6. Makonnen says he wants to change the world. What do you think he means by that?

7. What would you like to do someday that would make a difference in the world?

8. How do you think Makonnen's mother feels about her son's accomplishments?

He's Young and Wired *(cont.)*

Directions: Look at the character web. Answer the questions.

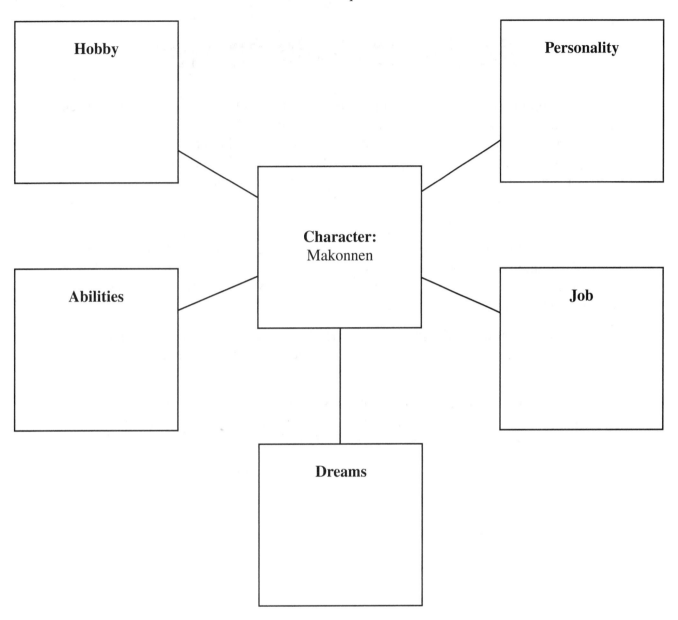

1. Complete the character web by adding information from the article about Makonnen.

2. How could this character web be used to help you with other writing you do?

Directions: Read the story.

Elephants Talk to Her

In 1984, biologist Katy Payne went to a zoo in Portland, Oregon. She wanted to listen to elephants. All she heard was the boom of giant feet hitting the ground. She also heard a few deep grunts. Payne had a feeling that the elephants were talking to one another. Then she remembered standing near the organ during choir practice as a kid. "When the organ played low notes, you could feel it much better than you could hear it." Payne felt a similar vibration when she stood near the elephants. "It occurred to me that they might be making very powerful, very low-pitched sounds."

Payne taped the elephants' sounds with a recorder. Then she played the tapes at fast speeds so that the sounds would be high enough for humans to hear. There they were! She could hear the elephants' voices! She spent the next seven years in Africa. She was listening to elephants in the wild.

Payne is an acoustic biologist. This is a scientist who studies the sounds of animals. She grew up on a farm in New York. "I was surrounded by animals," she recalls. "I just listened."

She began studying whale communication as soon as she graduated from college. Whales also use sounds with different meanings to communicate over long distances. But whales string sounds together to make a pattern. Elephants use each sound separately.

What are the elephants saying? "Most of the calls are group calls," she says. "I think they mean, 'We're here.' "

But elephants can no longer say, "We're here," in many parts of Africa. They've been hunted for their ivory tusks. They have been crowded out of their homes. Payne thinks that more people should open their ears to the language of elephants. Then more people would want to protect them. "Elephants will speak for themselves, if you give them a chance," she says.

Elephants Talk to Her (cont.)

Directions: Answer these questions. You may look at the story.

1. What animal does Payne study?

2. Why couldn't she hear the elephant sounds at first?

3. What did Payne remember about the organ? How does this relate to elephants?

4. How does an acoustic biologist's work help animals?

5. How are the languages of elephants and whales similar and different?

6. Payne thinks the elephants are saying, "We're here!" If the elephants could speak our language, what do you think they would say to us?

7. How can people help the elephants?

8. What is the purpose of this story?

Elephants Talk to Her *(cont.)*

Directions: Look at the diagrams. Answer the questions.

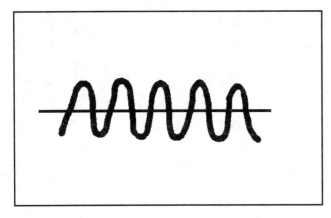

high-frequency sound wave

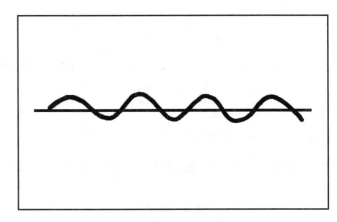

low-frequency sound wave

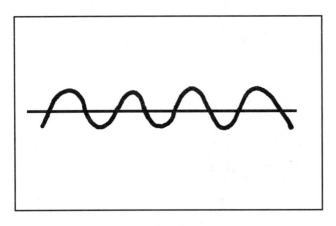

loud

soft

The sound waves of high-pitched sounds are fast and close together. The sound waves of low-pitched sounds are slow and farther apart.

The sound waves of loud sounds have higher and lower peaks than those of soft sounds.

1. If you could see the sound waves of an elephant noise, how would it compare to the sound waves of a human voice?

2. What would the sound waves of a mouse look like? Think about the pitch and the loudness.

3. Draw the sound waves that might be made by a large bird.

The Fossil Finder

When Sam Girouard was 8 years old, he went to Alabama. He was going to visit his grandmother. They explored an old mine. What they found changed his life forever. "It was just packed with fossils," says Sam.

Sam has been hunting fossils ever since. At age 16, he is now a respected paleontologist. He even helped a team from a Canadian museum. They dug up a T-rex skeleton.

One of Sam's most exciting discoveries required hours of careful reconstruction work. "I found these little shiny fragments of bone," he says. "I realized that what I had was a complete tyrannosaur tooth in about five dozen pieces. So I spent the entire day on my hands and knees, picking up all these little tiny pieces and gluing them together. By the end of the day, I had my tyrannosaur tooth."

In a gravel pit in Washington state he made another find. It was the wrist bone of a mastodon. Tests showed that it was millions of years old.

Sam spent his summer carefully chipping away at an ancient lake bed. He found raindrop fossils. He also found a fossilized wing of an extinct biting fly. "Those are extremely rare," he says.

Sam writes for professional journals. He doesn't include his age in his reports. Other paleontologists are surprised to learn that he is so young. "I'm afraid that if people first know I was a kid, my work wouldn't be taken seriously," says Sam. "I want people to see that I'm doing solid science, and then they can hear about my age."

The Fossil Finder (cont.)

Directions: Answer these questions. You may look at the story.

1. What did Sam and his grandmother explore?

2. What did Sam find in the mine?

3. How did the discovery change his life?

4. What was the condition of the tyrannosaur tooth he found?

5. Draw a picture of the how you think the tooth looked once Sam glued it together.

6. How do you think Sam knew that he had found fossils and not just rocks?

7. What does Sam mean when he says he's afraid people won't take him seriously if they know his age?

8. What do you think a professional journal is?

9. Rewrite the last paragraphs without using Sam's exact words.

The Fossil Finder (cont.)

Directions: Look at the picture. Answer the questions.

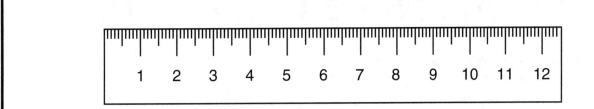

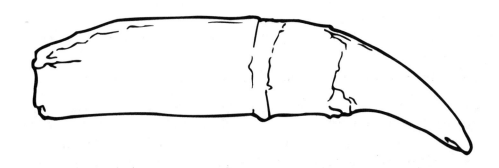

(**Note:** The ruler represents inches but is shown smaller than the actual size.)

1. Why is there a ruler above the T-rex tooth?

2. The tooth is very pointy. What do you think the T-rex ate?

3. What is a common object that is about the same length as the T-rex tooth?

Hot on Lewis and Clark's Trail

Nobody likes a litterbug. But historians wish that Lewis and Clark had left more behind. They traveled across the country nearly 200 years ago. It was a trip from Missouri to the Pacific. But it's hard to tell where they stopped on their trip.

Today, many people are hot on the trail of the explorers. They hope to answer many questions about these scouts of the West.

In 1803, President Thomas Jefferson asked Lewis to go exploring. He was hired to inspect the Louisiana Purchase. This was a huge area of land. America was about to buy it from France. He hoped to find a waterway between the Mississippi River and the Pacific. This would help with trade.

Lewis made the trip with his best friend. He and Clark left St. Louis in May, 1804. They never found the waterway. But they became the first U.S. citizens to see many of America's wonders. They saw the Great Plains. They saw the Rocky Mountains and the Pacific. They faced many perils. There were bear attacks and bitter cold. In Montana, they carried heavy canoes for weeks around waterfalls. They had to walk through the hot sun. At times, they were very hungry. Some days, they had to eat their pack horses.

They reached the Pacific. It took 500 days and 4,000 miles. "Ocian in view! O! the joy!" Clark wrote in his journal. (He was a terrible speller.)

The explorers kept maps and diaries. They wrote about 122 kinds of animals and 178 plants. They also wrote about many native tribes. But, they left barely a trace at their campsites. That makes it hard for historians to say, "Lewis and Clark were right here!"

Scientist Ken Karsmizki and others hope to pin down such facts. They are digging in the soil at Great Falls and Fort Clatsop. This is where the pair rested before making their separate ways home. Beads and gun ammunition were recently found at Fort Clatsop. More tests are needed to prove they belonged to Lewis and Clark.

The 200th anniversary of the journey is coming soon. People will have plenty of chances to learn about the pioneers. PBS will show a film about two men who retraced the trip. A Lewis and Clark museum will open in Great Falls. Celebrations along the trail are in the works.

Hot on Lewis and Clark's Trail (cont.)

Directions: Answer these questions. You may look at the story.

1. Who asked Lewis to go on the exploration?

2. How did Lewis and Clark know each other before the trip?

3. What do historians wish they could find?

4. How do you think a waterway between the Mississippi and the Pacific would have helped trade?

5. Explain the importance of the explorers describing the plants and animals they saw.

6. In what way do you think the maps and diaries were helpful to others?

7. If you were to go on an exploration, what kinds of supplies would you bring?

8. Why do you think this exploration is still celebrated today?

Hot on Lewis and Clark's Trail *(cont.)*

Directions: Read the journal excerpts. Answer the questions.

May 24, 1804

Passing near the southern shore, the bank fell in so fast as to oblige us to cross the river instantly, between the northern side and a sandbar which is constantly moving and banking with the violence of the current. The boat struck on it and would have upset immediately, if the men had not jumped into the water and held her, til the sand washed from under her.

June 15, 1804

. . . the river being very high, the sandbars were so rolling and numerous, and the current so strong, that we were unable to stem it even with the oars added to our sails; this obliged us to go nearer the banks, which were falling in, so that we could not make, though the boat was occasionally towed, more than fourteen miles.

July 12, 1804

The commanding officers, Capts. M. Lewis & W. Clark, constituted themselves a court martial for the trial of such persons as are guilty of capital crimes, and under the rules and articles of war punishable by DEATH. Alexander Willard was brought forward charged with "lying down and sleeping on his post" whilst a sentinal . . . . To this charge the prisoner pleads guilty of lying down, and not guilty of going to sleep. The court after duly considering the evidence aduced, are of opinion that the prisoner Alexdr. Willard is guilty of every part of the charge exhibited against him. It being a breach of the rules and articles of war do sentence him to receive one hundred lashes, on his bare back, at four different times in equal proportion, and order that the punishment commence this evening at sunset, and continue to be inflicted every evening until completed.

July 20, 1804

For a month past the party have been troubled with boils, and occasionally with the dysentery. These boils were large tumores which broke out under the arms, on the legs, and, generally, in the parts most exposed to action, which sometimes became too painful to permit the men to work. This disorder . . . has not affected the general health of the party, which is quite as good, if not better, than that of the same number of men in any other situation.

August 20, 1804

. . . we had the misfortune to lose one of our sergeants, Charles Floyd. He was yesterday seized with a bilious colic, and all our care and attention were ineffectual to relieve him. A little before his death, he said to Captain Clark, "I am going to leave you." His strength failed him as he added, "I want you to write me a letter," but he died with a composure which justified the high opinion [we] had formed of his firmness and good conduct. He was buried on the top of the bluff with the honors due to a brave soldier.

---

1. What were some of the dangers encountered on the expedition?

2. What crime is described in the journal? What was the punishment?

3. Put yourself in Lewis and Clark's shoes. Would you have been able to manage this expedition as well as they did? Why?

The Next Wave of Energy

Think of all the ways you used electricity today. Did you turn on a light this morning? Did you listen to the radio? Did you watch TV? All these things use electric power.

Where does this power come from? In most places in the world, it comes from burning fuels. These fuels are gas, coal, and oil. Big factories called power plants burn these fuels. That makes electricity.

Gas, coal, and oil are called fossil fuels. They are formed deep in the earth. This happens from the breakdown of animals and plants that lived millions of years ago. It takes that long for fossil fuels to form.

Fossil fuels have been the world's main source of energy a long time, but burning them gives off dirty gases. This is the main cause of pollution. Scientists have been looking for cleaner ways to light our lamps and heat our homes. They've found answers. They are blowing in the wind and shining in sunlight.

On April 22, people take time to think about the environment. This is called Earth Day. In some cities, Earth Day is every day. They use the sun and the wind for energy.

Using the power of the sun can be tricky. Scientists are still trying to figure out the best ways to catch sunlight and turn it into electricity.

In Japan, companies are making a special type of house. It has special roof tiles to absorb sunshine. The tiles work very well. They can make enough electricity for an entire family! And they are not too expensive to make. About 70,000 of these homes will be built in the next few years.

Windmills are also a source of energy. They have been used for hundreds of years. Modern windmills have lightweight blades that can catch more wind than ever before. "Windmills are taking an old technology and making it work today," says Jim Marston.

New windmills are popping up all over the U.S., Europe, and Asia. Denmark gets 6% of its electricity from wind power.

Our supply of fossil fuels is limited. But the energy we can get from the sun and the wind is endless!

The Next Wave of Energy (cont.)

Directions: Answer these questions. You may look at the story.

1. What is the main idea of this article?

2. What are three fuels that are burned to make power?

3. Why are fossil fuels a limited resource?

4. What are two unlimited sources of energy?

5. How can you help to take care of the environment?

6. What does the author mean by saying the answers are blowing in the wind and shining in the sun?

7. Why is it better to use power from the sun and wind?

8. If you could plan your own town, what three things would you do to help the environment? Be sure to include at least one idea about energy.

9. Describe a town that is making efforts to conserve the Earth's resources.

10. Write three reasons to support the use of power from the wind and sun.

The Next Wave of Energy (cont.)

Directions: Look at the picture diagram. Answer the questions.

1. How is this illustration related to the article?

2. Think about one room of your house. Write all the different ways that electricity is used in that room.

The Wolf Packs Are Back

For hundreds of years, wolves roamed the West. But when white settlers came in the 1800s, they feared them. Wolves often killed sheep and cattle.

To help farmers, the government paid to kill wolves. By the early 1930s, all of the wolves in Yellowstone National Park were gone.

Killing the wolves had a big effect on the animals and plants. Coyotes and elk are hunted by wolves. With the wolves gone, these animals grew in numbers. Plants that are eaten by elk began to disappear. Some elk starved. The government decided to bring wolves back to Yellowstone. It trapped some in Canada. The wolves were moved to the park. The goal is to put nature back into balance.

Not everyone was glad to see the wolves return. Farmers near the park were angry. The wolves have killed some sheep and cattle.

Some people think returning the wolves was against the law. A judge agreed with them. The judge said the wolves should be removed.

Many experts are fighting the judge's decision. The wolves have helped the park. Native plants are growing because there are fewer elk eating them. Beavers, which eat these plants, are also helped. Animals from the grizzly bear to the carrion beetle are doing well.

The wolves have a good friend named Bruce Babbitt. He is in charge of national parks. Babbitt says, "I will fight with everything I have to keep the wolves in Yellowstone." Anyone who cares about wildlife should join this fight.

The Wolf Packs Are Back (cont.)

Directions: Answer these questions. You may look at the story.

1. What did the wolves hunt?

2. Who paid to have wolves killed?

3. Explain what happened to the elk when the wolves were gone.

4. Imagine that you are a farmer in the Yellowstone area. Write a letter to the government expressing your concerns about the wolves.

5. Make a list of good things and bad things about bringing the wolves back to Yellowstone.

6. How does a national park help animals?

7. What does it mean when nature is out of balance?

8. Why is Babbitt a friend to wolves?

9. What is the main message of this story?

The Wolf Packs Are Back (cont.)

Directions: Look at the food chain. Answer the questions.

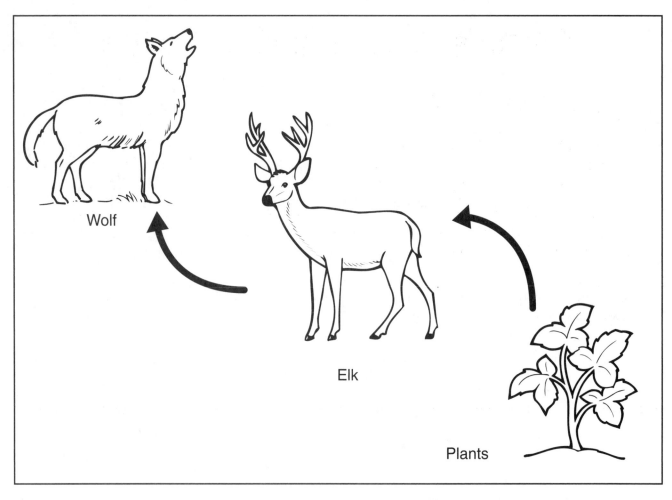

1. If there are no wolves to kill the elk, the elk population increases. What happens to the plants the elk eat?

2. If the plants are eaten by other animals as well, what would happen to those animals?

3. Wolves help nature to stay in balance. What does that mean?

Directions: Read the story.

China's Dam Is a Good Idea

China's Yangtze River is beautiful. But the river floods. The floods have killed many people. Now a new dam will stop these floods. It will also create electricity.

In 1997, China took a big step with the river. They dumped rocks into parts of it. They were getting ready to build a dam. It will be finished in 2009. It will be the biggest in the world. It will stop flooding. It will turn the water's energy into electricity.

Some people don't want the dam. A long lake will be formed by it. It will swallow up villages. Millions of people must move. The dam will ruin the homes of giant pandas, river dolphins, and other rare animals.

Still, the dam will do more good than harm. More electricity will help make new businesses. The people who must move are the ones put in danger by the floods. Some wildlife habitats will be destroyed, but many more will stay. Progress often causes problems. The Three Gorges Dam is a great example of progress!

China's Dam Is a Good Idea (cont.)

Directions: Answer these questions. You may look at the story.

1. What is the problem with the Yangtze River?

2. What can solve the flooding problem?

3. What will the dam be able to create?

4. Why are some people upset about the dam?

5. Who will benefit from the dam's electricity?

6. What does the word *progress* mean?

7. How could the dam change the environment in a bad way?

8. Imagine that you are a person against building the dam. Write a letter explaining your position.

9. Draw two pictures: one of the Yangtze River area before the dam and one after.

China's Dam Is a Good Idea *(cont.)*

Directions: Look at the diagram. Answer the questions.

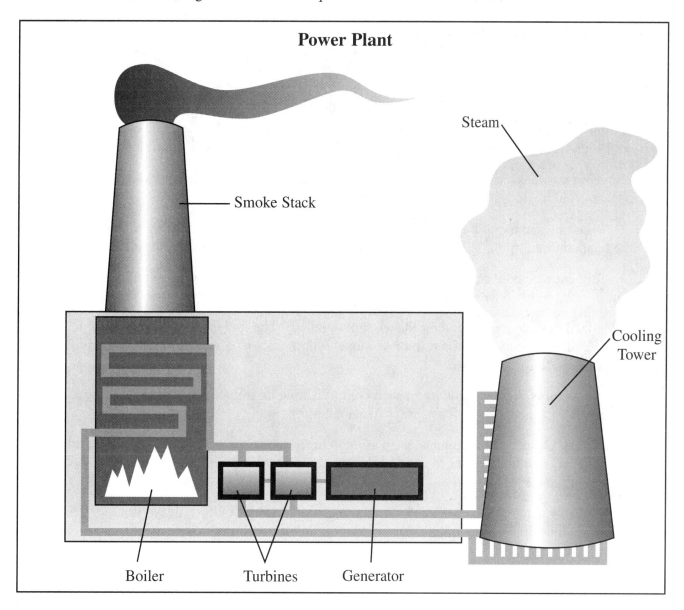

Power Plant

Steam

Smoke Stack

Cooling
Tower

Boiler   Turbines   Generator

1. What do you think is used to spin the turbines in a dam?

2. A dam holds back a lot of water. How would this affect the force of the water going through the dam?

The Big Chill

How cold was it in Alaska in February 1999? Well, when Ben Dallin threw a panful of boiling water into the air, it never came back down. "It just froze into fog and made a really cool sound," says Ben. In Ben's town of McGrath, it was 62 degrees below zero!

For two weeks, an icy chill covered Alaska. Temperatures dropped as low as –77 degrees. High winds make it feel even colder.

Alaskans are use to bad weather. Schools hardly ever close due to the cold. Only when the temperature dips to –20 degrees are students excused from outdoor recess.

But extreme cold causes problems. "It's hard to talk because your lips kind of go numb," says Abbe Skinner.

Machines can go numb, too. Planes can't take off. The fuel thickens up in the cold. Heating oil gets gunky. It's hard to make stoves work. Cars won't start, so people bring car batteries inside for the night.

Snow turns powdery and dry in such cold. Walking on it makes a weird squeaking noise. "It sounds like Styrofoam," says Arianna Solie.

Wood, plastic, and even metal snap as the temperature plummets. Trees crack and fall over. Pipes burst when water freezes inside them. One boy tried to start a snowmobile and the key broke off!

Becky Campbell thinks it's a good idea to go outside even in the coldest weather. "It's nice to be outside," she says. "It's part of Alaska. I don't let it get in my way."

The Big Chill *(cont.)*

Directions: Answer these questions. You may look at the story.

1. Why did the water freeze when Ben threw it into the air?

2. What else did Ben describe about what happened when he threw the water into the air?

3. Draw a picture of what Ben did.

4. Why aren't Alaskans bothered by cold weather?

5. What happens to fuel in cold weather? Why is this a problem?

6. Why do people bring their car batteries in for the night?

7. Think about the things you keep outside your house. What things would be damaged by extreme cold?

8. How do you think people in Alaska prepare for the freezing cold months?

9. Summarize the story using three sentences.

The Big Chill (cont.)

Directions: Look at the chart. Answer the questions.

	When you find yourself in very cold conditions, there are four key things to remember. They begin C-O-L-D.
Clean	Keep your clothes and body clean. Dirt decreases insulation in clothing. Washing helps avoid common skin rashes that can develop in very cold weather.
Overheated	Do not become overheated. This will make you sweat. The sweat will make your clothes damp, and damp clothes lose their ability to insulate. Sweating also cools a body down.
Loose Layers	Tight clothing restricts the flow of blood, and that cools a person down. Air between layers also adds extra layers of insulation. Several loose layers are better than one equally thick one.
Dry	Keep your clothing dry. Dry clothing provides insulation that wet clothing cannot.

1. What are some important things to keep in mind when you are in very cold conditions?

2. Why is getting wet a problem in very cold weather?

3. If you moved to McGrath, Alaska, what kinds of clothing would you be sure to have?

Directions: Read the story.

Winds of Destruction

The howling winds and sheets of rain came first. Palm trees were pounded by wind and rain. They bent over and touched the ground. Roofs lifted off buildings. Water flooded roads. Huge waves sent boats crashing into one another.

Next came the calm weather. The sun was bright and the skies were clear and blue. The damage could be seen. Electric power lines, trees, and pieces of homes were scattered everywhere.

This scene was played over and over again. It was Hurricane George. It roared through the islands of the Caribbean. Then it headed to Florida. The hurricane destroyed everything in its path.

Not an inch of Puerto Rico was spared from the storm. Its 110-mile-an-hour winds ripped up power lines and roofs. "This thing was a monster," said Pedro Juan Morales. His home was badly damaged. But he was luckier than most. The storm left many houses without electricity or running water. Many people were homeless.

The storm lashed into Florida. People were told to leave their homes. They needed to find shelter. One woman said, "When I return, I may not have a home."

George was blamed for billions of dollars' worth of damage. It also killed more than 300 people.

Winds of Destruction *(cont.)*

Directions: Answer these questions. You may look at the story.

1. Name three locations the hurricane hit.

2. What was the cost of the damage?

3. What is a hurricane?

4. What can a hurricane do?

5. Describe the way you think a city might look after a hurricane.

6. What do you think could be done to protect a home from a hurricane?

7. Why did people have to leave their homes?

8. Why does the author say Pedro Juan Morales was lucky? Do you agree? Why or why not?

9. What is the main idea of the article?

Winds of Destruction *(cont.)*

Directions: Look at the diagram. Answer the questions.

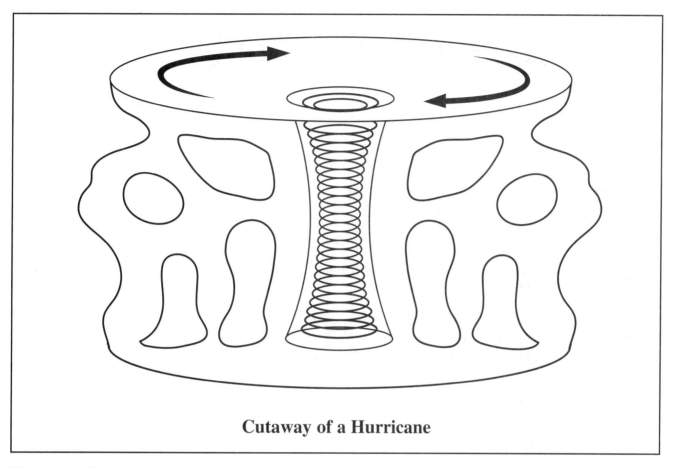

Cutaway of a Hurricane

The center of a hurricane is very calm, but the outer portions of a hurricane are violent and cause horrible destruction.

1. What do you think makes the center of a hurricane calm?

2. What does the spiral in the center of the diagram represent?

3. What do the arrows tell you about the hurricane?

Swept Away by Mitch

A little boy named Juan Pablo met President Clinton. He spoke softly. He said, "I lost my whole family. I miss them, my mama and my papa."

Juan is from Nicaragua. His village was hit by Hurricane Mitch. The heavy rains caused mud slides. The mud buried farms. It buried homes. Juan had to be rescued. He was buried in mud up to his neck. He was stuck for two days. Now he lives in a tent camp. A thousand other people live there, too.

President Clinton visited Juan's ruined village. He brought some money and supplies.

In Central America, the effects of Hurricane Mitch are still felt. The storm killed 9,000. It caused $10 billion in damage.

Many children died. Those who lived have found it hard to return to normal life. Homeless teenagers are drifting north toward Mexico. They are looking for work and a place to live. Many kids are out of school. That's because the buildings are being used as emergency housing.

The U.S. and other countries have sent some money to help Central America. The area needs even more help. The President has asked Congress for $956 million more. Congress has not yet approved it. While Congress is deciding, people are dying. We need to help one another. We need to help the people in Nicaragua.

Swept Away by Mitch *(cont.)*

Directions: Answer these questions. You may look at the story.

1. What is the name of the hurricane?

2. What did Juan Pablo lose in the hurricane?

3. What happened to Juan Pablo?

4. Why do the people live in camps now?

5. If you could help the people in Juan Pablo's town, what would you do?

6. How do you think Juan Pablo was able to survive for two days in the mud?

7. What do you think would need to be done to repair a town destroyed by rain and mudslides?

8. Why do you think it is taking so long to approve the money to be given to Nicaragua?

9. What is the message of this article?

Swept Away by Mitch (cont.)

Directions: Look at the illustrations. Answer the questions.

The Formation of a Hurricane

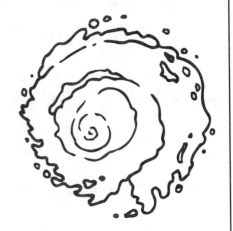

Several storms come together in the same area.

The storms gather together and make a tropical storm.

A hurricane is formed.

Hurricanes form over warm waters. Water vapor pushing up from the surface of the ocean makes hurricanes more intense.

1. During what time of year do you think most hurricanes form? Why?

2. Which areas of the United States do you think are relatively safe from hurricanes?

3. What do you think is the difference between a tropical storm and a hurricane?

Dino Eggs by the Dozen

It was more than 70 million years ago. A group of female dinosaurs roamed along a riverbank in South America. They were going to lay their eggs there. There were thousands of eggs! One by one, the baby dinosaurs started to hatch.

Then a giant flood washed over the land. They were lost forever.

Well, not quite forever. In November, 1998, a group of scientists uncovered something. They found the eggs and babies.

Scientists were in a field. It was covered with rocks the size of grapefruits. They took a closer look. The "rocks" were really dinosaur eggs. "There were thousands of eggs all over the place," says Luis Chiappe, a team leader.

The eggs belonged to small dinosaurs. They had long necks and ate plants. They are called titanosaurs.

Of course, these dinosaurs were not really small. An adult titanosaur was more than 50 feet long. Babies were about 15 inches long. That's "the size of a small poodle," says Chiappe.

The flood buried the eggs in mud. The mud helped preserve the babies still inside the eggshells. One egg held 32 teeth. Each tooth is small enough to fit inside this capital "O." Others held patches of scaly skin.

Chiappe and his team returned to the area. They hoped to answer more questions. They wanted to know whether the mama dinosaurs made careful nests or laid their eggs just anywhere. With so many eggs yet to be studied, those answers may be just waiting to hatch.

Dino Eggs by the Dozen *(cont.)*

Directions: Answer these questions. You may look at the story.

1. On what continent were the dinosaurs roaming the riverbank?

2. What happened to the eggs and newly hatched babies?

3. Why weren't the eggs and babies really lost forever?

4. Describe in detail what the scientists first saw in the field when they discovered the eggs.

5. Why do you think the scientists want to learn more about these dinosaurs?

6. How was this discovery helpful to scientists?

7. What would have happened to the babies if mud had not preserved them?

8. If the floods had not come, what do you think would have happened to these dinosaurs?

9. Is the purpose of this article to entertain, to inform, or to persuade? Explain your answer.

Dino Eggs by the Dozen *(cont.)*

Directions: Look at the map. Answer the questions.

1. On what continent were the dinosaur eggs found?

2. Why are there two maps shown in the illustration?

3. About how far away was the fossil-egg field from Buenos Aires?

A Cereal Shake-Up

The Post Cereal Company is about to give cereal lovers a treat. The good news is lower prices. Post said that it will cut the cost of its cereals about a dollar a box.

That's great news for shoppers. People have been complaining about the high price of cereal for years. Cereal in a box costs only about 50¢ to make. Boxes often sell for $4 or more.

The steep prices have made people wonder. More than 85% of cereal sold in the U.S. is made by four companies. Members of Congress want to find out if these companies are secretly agreeing to keep prices high. So far, no one has looked into this.

The cost of cereal includes more than just the flakes or O's you eat. The basic ingredients are similar in every box. Cereal is made of grains and sugar. So big cereal makers work hard to convince buyers that their brands are special.

These companies try to catch your eye. They create colorful boxes with cartoon characters on the front. They put games on the back. Sometimes they put prizes inside. TV ads also attempt to get your interest. Ads and fancy boxes cost money. That adds to the cereal's price.

The Post company decided to make a change. They knew that people were angry about high cereal prices. But Post isn't cutting prices just to be nice. It hopes that its lower prices will get people to buy their cereal.

A Cereal Shake-Up *(cont.)*

Directions: Answer these questions. You may look at the story.

1. What are people angry about?

2. How much does it cost to make a box of cereal?

3. What do cereal companies do that makes the cereal more expensive?

4. Describe in detail a box of your favorite cereal. Be sure to write about the bright colors and illustrations used to attract attention.

5. Why is Post planning to lower prices?

6. How much profit is made on a box of cereal?

7. Why would all of the companies secretly keep cereal prices high?

8. Why do you think people keep buying expensive cereal?

9. How do you think Post's lower prices will change cereal sales and choices?

A Cereal Shake-Up *(cont.)*

Directions: Look at the graph. Answer the questions.

Breakfast Food Sales

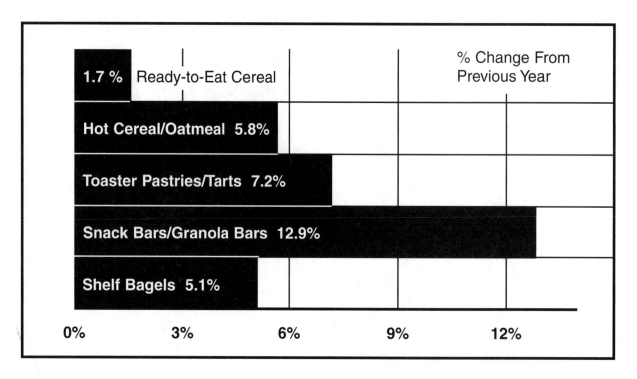

1. Thinking about the busy lives of people in our country, what does this graph indicate to you?

2. What does this graph indicate about the reason for the high prices of cereal?

3. Do you think people buy less cereal because it is expensive? Or do you think that cereal is more expensive because fewer people are buying it?

Directions: Read the story.

A Spooky Friend

The sun sets below the horizon. The wind blows leaves around your feet. Suddenly a vampire bat swoops down to suck your blood!

OK, catch your breath. Scary stories about bats have been around for a long time. In real life, bats hardly ever hurt people. These furry, flying mammals are really very helpful.

Bats eat bugs. Bugs hurt farmers crops. Bats feast on insect pests and help farmers. There are 20 million Mexican free-tailed bats near San Antonio, Texas. They eat up 250 tons of insects every night! Bats also snack on flies and mosquitoes that can get in your food.

Bats help the desert, too. They carry pollen from cactus to cactus and spread the seeds around. Birds and other desert animals depend on cactus plants for food.

Actually bats should be afraid of people. Today many kinds of bats are endangered.

Some people fear bats. They burn them out of caves or bury them inside mines. Thomas Kunz is a biologist. He says, "They think every bat is a vampire bat, and they kill all they can find."

A Spooky Friend *(cont.)*

Directions: Answer these questions. You may look at the story.

1. What do bats eat?

2. How many tons of insects can bats eat in a night?

3. How do bats help farmers?

4. Describe several helpful things that bats do.

5. If the bats in Texas eat 250 tons of insects a night, how many would they eat in a week?

6. Write a letter to persuade people to appreciate bats. Be sure to include facts from the article to support your argument.

7. If all bats disappeared, how would that hurt the environment?

8. Summarize the article using only five sentences.

A Spooky Friend *(cont.)*

Directions: Look at the illustration. Answer the questions.

Most bats use echolocation to find their way in the dark and to catch insects. The illustration below shows the sound waves that are made when a bat makes noises.

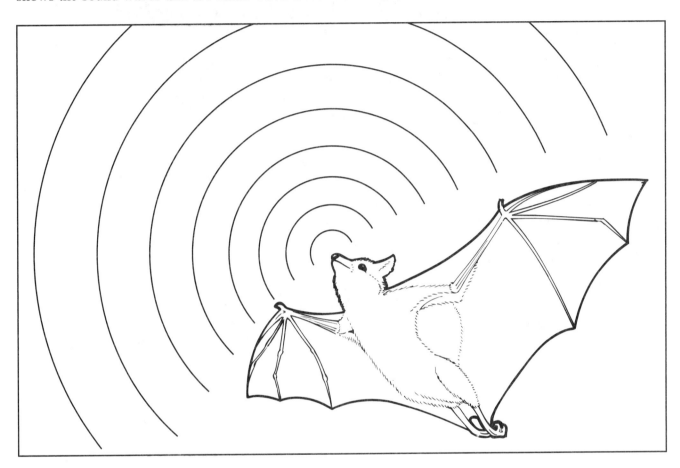

1. How do you think a bat uses sound to "see" in the dark?

2. What is an echo?

3. What do you think happens when a bat uses echolocation?

Directions: Read the story.

Top Tasters

Do you think broccoli tastes bitter? Don't blame the cook! Researchers say that what tastes good or bad can depend on the taster's genes. Genes are the chemical instructions that make you who you are. They determine the color of your eyes. They determine the shape of your nose and face. Now scientists know even more. Genes also determine how many taste buds are on your tongue.

One-quarter of people are supertasters. They have many taste buds. Because of this, they find the flavor of some foods unpleasantly strong. Cabbage seems very bitter to them. Chocolate seems way too sweet. One-quarter are nontasters with few taste buds. Half are medium tasters who enjoy most foods.

But don't use your genes as an excuse to skip your veggies! For vitamins and other nutrients, vegetables are always in good taste.

Top Tasters *(cont.)*

Directions: Answer these questions. You may look at the story.

1. What are the chemical instructions for our bodies?

2. What are supertasters?

3. Why can't some people taste very much?

4. If you were a supertaster, what kinds of foods do you think you would like?

5. What kinds of foods could nontasters eat that medium tasters wouldn't like?

6. Why is it important to eat your fruits and vegetables?

7. What could happen to your body if you didn't eat fruits and vegetables?

8. What is the main idea of this article?

Top Tasters *(cont.)*

Directions: Look at the graph. Answer the questions.

Top 5 Fruits

The graph shows how many of these juicy favorites the average American eats in one year.

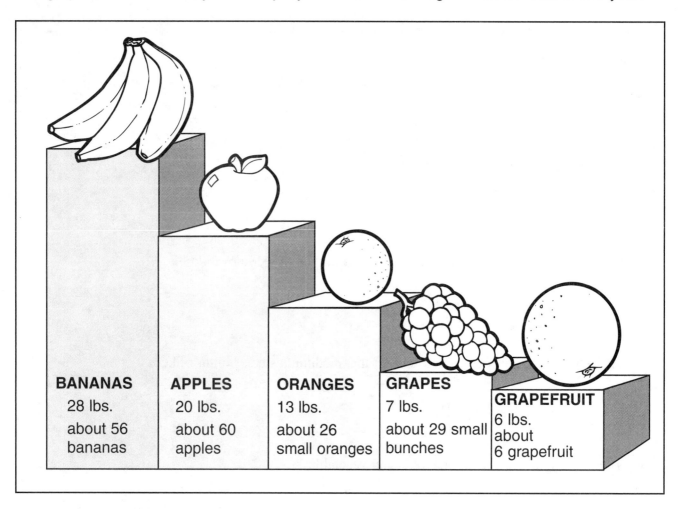

BANANAS
28 lbs.
about 56 bananas

APPLES
20 lbs.
about 60 apples

ORANGES
13 lbs.
about 26 small oranges

GRAPES
7 lbs.
about 29 small bunches

GRAPEFRUIT
6 lbs.
about 6 grapefruit

1. What is the purpose of the graph?

2. How are your favorite tastes similar or unlike those on the graph?

Student Achievement Graph

Passage Title	Number of Questions Correctly Answered							
	1	2	3	4	5	6	7	8

Answer Key

Page 17
1. It was flooded.
2. El Niño
3. flooding, home destruction, mud slides, power outages, etc.
4. Responses will vary.
5. Responses will vary. Answers should include storm forecasts.
6. Responses will vary.
7. Responses will vary.
8. Responses will vary.

Page 18
1. Responses may include weakening or shifting winds, movement of warm water eastward, increased thunderstorm activity eastward, thermocline depression in the east, and rainfall shifts.
2. Responses will vary but may suggest that research can help people to predict El Niño conditions and therefore be better prepared for them.

Page 20
1. Sweden
2. It's made of ice.
3. a certificate
4. They receive snowsuits and mummy-style sleeping bags.
5. Responses will vary.
6. Responses will vary.
7. Responses will vary.
8. Responses will vary.
9. Responses will vary.

Page 21
1. Responses will vary, but they should include details about how a person can stay warm enough for survival in such cold conditions (for example, thermal underwear, down-filled and waterproof clothing, waterproof thermal blankets, etc.)
2. Responses will vary.

Page 23
1. Lunar Prospector
2. to the moon
3. It will travel around the moon. It will study the moon's surface. It will also determine of what the moon is made.
4. Apollo landed on the moon.
5. Responses will vary.
6. Responses will vary.
7. Responses will vary. Answers should include the fact that a water supply might make life possible.
8. Responses will vary.

Page 24
1. The outline does not mention past space travel or the idea that finding a water supply would make life on the moon possible.
2. An outline is helpful for planning and organizing before beginning to draft the writing.

Page 26
1. Vikings
2. a knarr or a big merchant ship with oars
3. He was going to sail the path of Leif Eriksson.
4. two
5. Responses will vary. Answers should include the differences among the equipment used.
6. the North Star
7. Responses will vary. Answers should include safety issues.

8. Birds need a place to land, so seeing birds means land is near.
9. Responses will vary.

Page 27
1. It shows the route that the crew sailed.
2. They headed north.
3. They wanted to follow the same route as Leif Eriksson.

Page 29
1. Dominican Republic (also Cuba)
2. 500 years old
3. Responses will vary.
4. the arrival of Columbus and other explorers
5. They took their land, spread diseases, and killed them.
6. Responses will vary.
7. Responses will vary.
8. Responses will vary.
9. Responses will vary. Answers might include that the people would have survived or that Columbus might not have made further discoveries.

Page 30
1. Florida
2. Responses will vary. Students might mention that these people lived very close to the United States and the two cultures encountered one another, thereby sharing some vocabulary.

Page 32
1. He traveled around the earth.
2. No one was with him.
3. They were able to learn about the effects of aging.
4. Responses will vary. Answers might include that no one of Glenn's age had ever before traveled in space.
5. Responses will vary. Answers should include the different spacecraft, crew members, and purposes of the trip.
6. Responses will vary.
7. Responses will vary.
8. Responses will vary.

Page 33
1. his hair color and his age
2. *Discovery* is larger and could hold more than *Friendship* 7 could.
3. The development of computers is evident.

Page 35
1. a new territory
2. Nunavut
3. It means "our land."
4. tundra, islands, and lakes
5. Responses will vary.
6. Responses will vary.
7. Responses will vary.
8. Responses will vary. Answers might include that the natives know about the needs of their own people.
9. Responses will vary. Answers might include that white men controlled the people and that they did not have the freedoms they wanted.

Page 36
1. They give facts about the land and the people. They also show the surrounding countries and bodies of water.
2. Responses will vary.

Page 38
1. Peru
2. a mummy (also statues, clothing, and headdresses)
3. It was frozen.
4. They can learn about the Incas' health.
5. They sacrificed people in religious ceremonies so that the gods would stop natural disasters.
6. Responses will vary. They probably thought it was an honor to save their people.
7. The heat from an erupting volcano melted the ice that buried the treasures.
8. Responses will vary.

Page 39
1. They found them in the southern part of Peru.
2. Responses will vary. Students might say that the mountain is at a high altitude where it is colder.

Page 41
1. The land is being cleared.
2. about 11,200
3. Brazil promised to enforce laws that protect the rain forest.
4. Responses will vary.
5. Responses will vary.
6. Deforestation is the burning or clearing of the forest plants and trees.
7. It was partially due to heavy rainfall.
8. Responses will vary.
9. Responses will vary.

Page 42
1. Loss of rain forest decreased.
2. Responses will vary.
3. Responses will vary. Students might say that it would continue to decrease because of the downward trend.

Page 44
1. "The Star-Spangled Banner"
2. Francis Scott Key wrote the song.
3. He saw the flag waving after a battle.
4. Time, light, pollution, and moist air damaged it.
5. Responses will vary.
6. Responses will vary. Answers might include that it represents the history of our country.
7. Responses will vary.
8. Responses will vary.

Page 45
1. Responses will vary.
2. They represent states or colonies.
3. The flag would have one more star added to it.

Page 47
1. a meteor shower
2. Some people were afraid. Some tried to catch them.
3. A meteor shower is caused when a comet passes by Earth.
4. Responses will vary.
5. 166 years
6. A comet passes near the sun. The ice heats up and pieces fall off. The pieces enter Earth's atmosphere. They catch fire.
7. Responses will vary.
8. Responses will vary.

Answer Key (cont.)

Page 48
1. Responses will vary. It provides more information.
2. Responses will vary.
3. Responses will vary. Students might say that meteors look like stars because they are on fire.

Page 50
1. Africa
2. on the Internet
3. He is the trip leader.
4. 250 miles a week
5. They can e-mail the team, ask questions, and offer suggestions.
6. Responses will vary.
7. Responses will vary.
8. Responses will vary.
9. Responses will vary.

Page 51
1. It travels up a conduit.
2. Answers will vary but should make comparisons between the volcano's throat and a person's throat.
3. Responses will vary.

Page 53
1. People want to increase their numbers and raise awareness about the problem.
2. Their numbers are shrinking.
3. Some fisherman still catch more than they should.
4. Responses will vary.
5. Responses will vary.
6. Female swordfish may be pregnant or they may not have had the chance to have babies.
7. In the 1950s, swordfish were caught with harpoons. Now they are caught by the hundreds on lines with many hooks.
8. Responses will vary. Answers should include that swordfish could become extinct.

Page 54
1. Responses will vary but should suggest that the numbers of fish in the ocean over time are decreasing due to the increasing numbers of fish being caught.
2. It is increasing every year.
3. Responses will vary.

Page 56
1. There weren't many trees in their area. They wanted to attract wildlife.
2. They hoped the trees would attract birds and other wildlife.
3. An indicator species is an animal that lives in an area, showing other animals it is good to live there, too.
4. Responses will vary.
5. Responses will vary.
6. Responses will vary.
7. Responses will vary.
8. Responses will vary.
9. Green trees will be more noticeable than brown dirt.

Page 57
1. Responses will vary. Information should come from the article.

Page 59
1. She works to get rid of land mines in the world. She received a Nobel Peace Prize.
2. It is an explosive that is underground.
3. The Nobel Peace Prize is awarded for work that helps people and helps to bring peace.
4. more than 26,000 people

5. Responses will vary.
6. Responses will vary.
7. Responses will vary.
8. Responses will vary. Answers should include her work to get rid of land mines and to get nations to agree not to use them.

Page 60
1. It shows the places in the world that are dangerous.
2. It shows specific countries that have land mines.
3. There aren't any land mines in the U.S. and Africa has many places with land mines.

Page 62
1. He is a photographer.
2. He got to take pictures at the World Series.
3. He is 15 years old.
4. It's amazing because he is so young.
5. Responses will vary.
6. Responses will vary.
7. He wanted to take a picture of a baseball coming straight at him and then breaking his camera without ruining his film. He was not able to get the shot.
8. Responses will vary.

Page 63
1. Responses will vary.
2. Responses will vary.
3. There is a lot to understand about the camera itself.

Page 65
1. itchy throat, runny nose, upset stomach, trouble breathing
2. The person could die.
3. They are not serving peanuts because many people have severe allergies to them.
4. Responses will vary. Answers should include that a person would have to be careful that peanuts or peanut oil are not being served or cooked. The person might have to wash his or her hands a lot.
5. A table where no one is eating food made with peanuts.
6. It means that no peanuts or peanut products are allowed anywhere in the school.
7. Responses will vary. Many foods are made with crushed peanuts, peanut butter, or peanut oil. These can't been seen, so a person might not know they are there.
8. Responses will vary. The person would have to check the ingredients in foods and be sure that he or she would not come in contact with peanuts.
9. Responses will vary.

Page 66
1. Allergens may be everywhere, so the allergic person is in constant danger of an allergic reaction.
2. It keeps the histimines from doing what they do, so the person won't be itchy and swollen, have breathing problems, or have his or her throat become restricted.
3. Responses will vary.

Page 68
1. He uploaded information to a Web site.
2. It's amazing because Makonnen is so young.
3. He is a government advisor in the field of high technology.
4. Responses will vary.
5. Responses will vary. Answers might include that it is important to learn to use

technology in order to get good jobs and to compete with the rest of the world.
6. Responses will vary.
7. Responses will vary.
8. Responses will vary.

Page 69
1. Responses will vary. Students should add that Makonnen works as an advisor, has great computer skills, likes to play computer games, and wants to design computer games someday.
2. Responses will vary.

Page 71
1. elephants
2. The sounds were too low for the human ear to hear.
3. She could feel the low notes better than she could hear them. She thought the elephants' voices might be low, too.
4. Responses will vary.
5. Both whales and elephants can communicate. Whales' sounds are strung together. Elephants' sounds are separate.
6. Responses will vary.
7. Responses will vary.
8. Responses will vary. Answers might include that the article provides information, tells about Payne's work, and attempts to persuade people to help save the elephants.

Page 72
1. The elephant sounds waves would be wider.
2. The mouse's sound waves would be close together and make a straighter line than a loud sound would.
3. The drawing will likely show loud sounds with a high pitch, but drawings will vary. Accept anything reasonable that uses the sound wave diagrams as a model.

Page 74
1. a mine
2. fossils
3. He became a paleontologist.
4. It was in pieces.
5. Responses will vary.
6. Responses will vary.
7. Responses will vary. They might not want to learn from him because he is just a kid.
8. Responses will vary. It is a magazine for professionals.
9. Responses will vary.

Page 75
1. It is there to show the size of the tooth.
2. The T rex ate meat.
3. Responses will vary. Of course, some students may answer "a ruler."

Page 77
1. the president
2. They were best friends.
3. More evidence about the exploration and exactly where the two traveled and rested.
4. Responses will vary, but they may suggest that a waterway would make moving trade from one area to another faster and easier.
5. People had never heard of many of the plants and animals. Lewis and Clark were able to provide educational information.
6. Responses will vary.
7. Responses will vary.
8. Responses will vary.

Answer Key (cont.)

Page 78
1. Answers should include (but are not limited to) two or more of the following: illness, death, crime, and forces of nature.
2. A sentinel is charged with lying down and sleeping at his post. His punishment is "to receive one hundred lashes, on his bare back, at four different times in equal proportion."
3. Responses will vary.

Page 80
1. The main idea is that it is better to generate energy from sun and wind than from fossil fuels.
2. gas, coal, and oil
3. They are made from plants and animals from millions of years ago. These resources can run out.
4. sun and wind
5. Responses will vary.
6. Responses will vary.
7. The sun and wind will never disappear. These resources will not run out.
8. Responses will vary.
9. Responses will vary.
10. Responses will vary.

Page 81
1. It shows many different ways that electricity is used in our homes.
2. Responses will vary.

Page 83
1. sheep and cattle
2. the government
3. There were no predators of the elk. Their numbers increased. The plants that the elk ate were eaten up and the elk began to starve.
4. Responses will vary.
5. Responses will vary. The list should include issues from those for and against the return of the wolves.
6. Responses will vary.
7. Responses will vary.
8. He is fighting to keep them in Yellowstone.
9. Wolves are a natural part of the environment and they should be allowed to stay.

Page 84
1. They disappear because they are all eaten.
2. They would starve because there is no more food.
3. Responses will vary.

Page 86
1. It floods.
2. building a dam
3. electricity
4. It will form a lake where towns are located, and it will destroy some animal habitats.
5. The people will benefit.
6. It means advancing or moving ahead.
7. Responses will vary, although students should mention that it will destroy habitats in the area.
8. Responses will vary.
9. Responses will vary.

Page 87
1. water
2. It would be extremely forceful. A lot of water pushes against the dam.

Page 89
1. It was really cold outside.
2. It turned into a fog and made a cool sound.
3. Responses will vary.
4. They have cold weather much of the time.
5. It gets thick and gunky. Machines won't work.
6. They bring them inside so the batteries will stay warm and their cars will run in the morning.
7. Responses will vary.
8. Responses will vary.
9. Responses will vary.

Page 90
1. You should remember to keep clean, not to become overheated, to wear loose layers, and to stay dry.
2. Wet clothing loses some of its ability to insulate, and therefore does not keep a person warm like it should.
3. Responses will vary but should include logical information regarding warm clothing with lots of layering ability.

Page 92
1. islands of the Caribbean, Florida, and Puerto Rico
2. billions of dollars
3. a storm with heavy rain and strong winds
4. A hurricane can destroy homes, break power lines, uproot trees, etc.
5. Responses will vary.
6. Responses will vary.
7. They needed to get to safety.
8. His house was damaged, but not destroyed. Opinions will vary.
9. Hurricane George was a terrible hurricane that cost billions of dollars of damage and took lives.

Page 93
1. Responses will vary.
2. the center or eye of the hurricane
3. It moves.

Page 95
1. Mitch
2. He lost his parents and his home.
3. He was buried in the mud for two days.
4. Their homes were destroyed.
5. Responses will vary.
6. Responses will vary.
7. Responses will vary.
8. Responses will vary.
9. The people of Nicaragua need our help.

Page 96
1. Responses will vary, but it is likely the students will say during the summer because hurricanes require warm water.
2. Areas far away from oceans are relatively safe.
3. A hurricane is far more intense than a tropical storm. It has more power and does more damage.

Page 98
1. South America
2. They were buried in a flood.
3. The fossils were found by scientists.
4. Rocks the size of grapefruit covered the field. Upon a closer look, they were discovered to be dino eggs.
5. Responses will vary.
6. Responses will vary.
7. They would have deteriorated.

8. Responses will vary.
9. The purpose is to inform. The author shares information about a topic. The author does not try to be funny and does not try to change the reader's opinion. He or she is just providing interesting information.

Page 99
1. They were found on the continent of South America.
2. They are a globe showing South America and a map of Argentina, which is in South America.
3. It is about 700 miles (1100 km) away.

Page 101
1. high cereal prices
2. about fifty cents
3. They make fancy boxes, include prizes and games, and run ads.
4. Responses will vary.
5. Their customers are angry, and the company wants to sell more cereal.
6. $3.50
7. Responses will vary.
8. Responses will vary.
9. Responses will vary.

Page 102
1. People like to eat quick and easy food for breakfast.
2. Responses will vary, but students may suggest that because cereal makes up a smaller portion of breakfast foods than do other items, perhaps the companies need to charge more to help pay expenses.
3. Responses will vary.

Page 104
1. insects
2. 250 tons
3. They eat insects that eat crops.
4. Responses may include eating insects and spreading pollen.
5. 1,750 tons
6. Responses will vary.
7. Responses will vary.
8. Responses will vary.

Page 105
1. Responses will vary.
2. Sound bounces off of a surface and sends the sound back to our ears.
3. The bat makes a sound and the sound waves bounce off nearby objects.

Page 107
1. genes
2. Supertasters are people who have lots of taste buds on their tongues.
3. They don't have very many taste buds.
4. Bland foods that aren't too spicy or too sweet.
5. Responses will vary.
6. Fruits and vegetables have vitamins and nutrients in them.
7. A person can get sick from not eating properly.
8. The article is about the tastes of different people and how that affects the foods they like and don't like.

Page 108
1. The graph shows favorite fruits and how much of each one the average American eats each year.
2. Responses will vary.